PRAISE FOR THE BOOK

"Dr Nia Thomas offers a compelling and insightful guide for leaders seeking to enhance their effectiveness by understanding the impact of their behaviour and actions. Dr Thomas provides a raw and honest perspective, encouraging leaders to step outside themselves and critically reflect on their leadership capabilities, gaps and potential. This book is a must-read for leaders aspiring to deepen their self-awareness and enhance their impact, whether they be an experienced manager or new to their leadership journey. Dr Thomas's blend of research-backed guidance and personal anecdotes creates a compelling narrative that will resonate with leaders striving to create positive change within their organisation."

T. Poore
Charitable-Sector CEO, Public-Sector Experienced

"A seemingly effortless journey through self-awareness that encourages the traveller to stop at the junctions of theory, practice, paradox and dilemma, destined in growing their leadership."

E. Piera
Leadership Development Specialist, Coach and Lecturer

"What sets this book apart is its foundation in extensive research and Dr Thomas's personal experiences, which enrich the content with authenticity and relatability. By weaving together theory and practical insights, the author creates a compelling narrative that resonates with leaders navigating their own leadership journeys."

"It is truly a treasure trove of knowledge, and I'm so impressed at how you have assimilated your personal research, that of others and podcast guest insights, along with examples of lived experience, to provide a hugely valuable, credible and engaging resource!"

"You have a real skill at taking academic research and concepts and communicating them in a way that is clear and accessible."

"Dr Thomas emphasizes the importance of introspection and self-awareness in creating environments that prioritise empathy, diversity and inclusivity."

"It works beautifully. I adore how you take your reader on a journey of discovery."

"I love your tone of voice – professional but approachable."

"A very eloquent writing style."

"Illuminating and valuable."

"Honest and refreshing."

THE SELF-AWARENESS SUPERHIGHWAY

CHARTING YOUR LEADERSHIP JOURNEY

Writing Coach: Steph Caswell
Copyeditor: Jessica Brown
Proofreader: Kerry Walters
Formatter: Zara Thatcher
Cover Designer: Liam Beattie

For those who want to care better for others and those who want to be better cared for by others.

CONTENTS

PREFACE

A Word from Your Journey Guide...

Why are you here, traveller?

Where are you going?

How will you get there?

Journey with me on the Self-Awareness Superhighway, which will guide, inform and empower you to form your own answers to each of these questions.

To discover why you are here, you'll explore the definition of self-awareness, what makes an effective leader and where leaders can be found in all organisations. You'll come to understand the importance of all these elements to you and how this knowledge will inform every single one of your relationships, current and future. You'll also be able to reflect on relationships past.

To help you decide where you are going and where to travel, you'll explore the nine CHARTABLE compass points of care, humility, authenticity, reflection, trust, adaptability, behaviour, listening and experience. You'll also tour the signposts and directions that will guide you, and the roadblocks and trip hazards that will obstruct you.

To chart your journey and determine the methods you'll use to travel, you'll delve into practices like mindfulness and journaling, and tests, tools and techniques like 360-degree reviews and leadership assessments. You'll also be gifted the Self-Awareness Compass Quiz, a unique addition to this book, developed especially for you. It will help you decide which of the nine compass directions you should travel in, with a little help from your friends.

Along the journey, you will share the road with me, your journey guide, and guests from *The Knowing Self Knowing Others Podcast*. Thoughts, ideas and experiences converge in this guide to bring academia to the office and wisdom to the workplace.

I hope your journey through this book will be enlightening and fulfilling. I hope it inspires you to be an ambassador for self-aware leadership in your organisation and beyond, raising awareness of awareness wherever you go. I hope it forms the topic of discussion by the watercooler and that the discussion motivates your colleagues to reflect on their skills, recognise their impact and regulate their behaviour.

But anyway, let's not dilly-dally any longer. The train is about to leave the station, the plane is taxiing up the runway, the ship is heading out of the harbour and the car is pulling off the drive.

Buckle up! I think you're going to enjoy the ride!

1. DEPARTURES

What's It All About?

Welcome to the Self-Awareness Superhighway!

I'm glad you're joining me on this learning journey to create kinder, more respectful and creative working relationships through reflection on hard and relational skills, recognition of impact and regulation of behaviour.

Life is a series of twists and turns along narrow country lanes, main roads and frantic motorways. You live your life, day to day, manoeuvring potholes, 90-degree bends and with other travellers in front, behind and to the side of you. You go about your business, focussed on your tasks and prioritising your most important people. You do your best to be your best and do your best for others.

Being purposefully reflective allows you the opportunity to elevate your perspective above all these daily tasks and gives you the chance to develop your self-awareness. It's a different time and space, where you give yourself a new vantage point to be objective and more considered about what you do and how you do it. Your unique journey along your superhighway will give you the opportunity to achieve that objective vantage point from which you can reflect on your skills, recognise your impact and self-regulate your behaviour. Your superhighway will give you the ability to journey through your leadership career with awareness, manoeuvre from a place of conscious decision making and build positive relationships with others, both now and into the future.

I love the London skyline and seeing it makes me happy. When I'm sitting in the passenger seat of the car, one of my most favourite things to do is Shard-spotting. The Shard has 72 floors and stands in the very centre of London. It's a pointy sliver of a building that looks like an icicle. You can see it from miles around, meaning that when you're travelling around Greater London and the neighbouring boroughs, you can spot it from elevated points, bridges, hilltops and high buildings.

Shard-spotting is a perfect metaphor for riding the Self-Awareness Superhighway. When I'm going about my business day to day, nipping to the supermarket for this evening's dinner and tomorrow's sandwiches, I need to keep my eyes on the road and concentrate on what I'm doing in the moment. I'm never going to have the opportunity to spot The Shard. I can only do that when I decide to sit in the passenger seat, actively look out the window, pay attention to the undulations in the road, have an idea of the direction to look and turn my head to see.

To develop your self-awareness, you'll need to do the same. Developing your self-awareness is an activity, not a passivity. You've got to get out there on your superhighway, raise your gaze and reflect, recognise and regulate.

But what is a superhighway anyway?

It's a multi-laned road where vehicles travel at high speed over long distances. As you journey through this book, your sense of your own superhighway will become clear. You may see it, hear it, smell it, feel it and you may even taste it! You will tap into all the senses available to you to experience it.

I've been on this journey for a few years now, and I can clearly visualise my superhighway. Mine is one of those sky-roads, raised above the trees, with a helicopter view of life below. It's a vantage point down to the river and the village and the London city skyline in the background. My vehicle is a little car-sized version of the silver caravan you've seen in movies, sometimes called an Airstream trailer, depending on which continent you live. My silver bullet hovers above the roadway and quietly speeds along, stopping at the command of my voice, chauffeured by a bodyless artificial intelligence that opens and closes my door and asks me if I've had a nice day. It's got 360-degree windows that allow me to see out across the landscape below and the superhighway all around. It's fluffy and comfortable inside, with room for a passenger or two.

By the end of this book, you too will have a clear vision of your superhighway and your mode of transport. You may be riding a bicycle, diving in a submarine, flying a personalised drone or hiking on foot. You might even change your vehicle from time to time. This guide will encourage you to explore different modes and be creative as you journey through the changing environments.

What about self-awareness? Well, self-awareness has two perspectives: self and others. 'You' is the 'self' that's on the journey. The 'others' are people you meet and spend time with along the way. People like me!

Let me explain.

You – the self – are on the journey of self-awareness. It's a never-ending journey that begins when you notice you have toes and ends when you take your final breath. It's a journey *of* self-awareness, not a journey *to* self-awareness. This guide will help you chart your very own map along your superhighway to various checkpoints, stop points and junctions as you travel between birth and shuffling off this mortal coil, all the while getting to know yourself and getting to know others.

The cycle of knowing self and knowing others gives you the chance to get to know yourself better through reflection on your skills and recognition of your impact on others. That then affords you the gift of being able to regulate and change your behaviour for both your benefit and the benefit of others. It's a big, never-ending, virtuous cycle of improvement. The wheels on the bus go round and round, and round, and round...

On your journey, you'll travel alongside others for a moment, a few days, a few months or maybe for the whole of your life. But their journey won't be the same as yours. Your journeys will align and cross but will never be identical. And in these instances when you interact, relate and work together, you'll be involved in an invisible volley of relationship behaviours with your family, friends, colleagues, frenemies, acquaintances and people you say "Excuse me" to as you pass in the doorway of the service station.

When I say 'behaviour', I simply mean the way we behave. There's no negative connotation to it here, unlike the social meaning it's gathered in everyday speak.

In the world of work and the function of leadership, every single one of your behaviours is going to be observed by someone. Everything you say, every move you make is noticed, observed, scrutinised, analysed and remembered. And it's going to come back to you. One day, in some way, that behaviour is going to make its way back to you. How you throw your behaviours out into the world has an impact, both on others and yourself. When The Police sang 'Every Breath You Take' in 1983, they were absolutely right!

Let's take this idea out onto the superhighway. You know who the considerate and inconsiderate drivers are. You've heard all about road rage and the life-defining impacts when drivers enter into the red mist and emerge having carried out verbal attacks on other road users. Do you find yourself embroiled in road rage incidents on your superhighway? Or are you the traveller that gives way and forgives people when their indicators "aren't working"? How are you throwing your behaviour around out there? And how is it coming back at you?

This is why you need to make conscious choices about what you put out into the world. You can only make conscious choices when you're aware of what you think, feel, value, believe, love, are biased towards, dislike and hate. And you can only do that by embarking on your journey of self-awareness!

The world is full of phrases that raise awareness of the impact of behaviour...

- Get a taste of your own medicine.
- What goes around comes around.
- You reap what you sow.

- People in glass houses shouldn't throw stones.
- There's always one – and if there isn't, it's probably you.

They exist because they're true!

What you'll notice about the Self-Awareness Superhighway is that not everyone will be on it and not everyone will spend as much time on it as you. Some may simply ride it for the length of a training course or a psychometric test and then turn off onto an A road or a B road. Some people will never get into their Airstream and hover along their superhighway. Some people will never know there's even a superhighway to be travelled or that there's a self to become aware of. Some may never realise they have an impact on others and that they have the ability to change that impact.

But you do, and that's why you're here!

Why I Wrote This Book

I wrote this book because you matter – because of the potential you have to make other people's work lives wonderful or miserable and the potential you have to make what you put out into the world ricochet back at you as twinkling unicorn glitter or six-inch nails. Unless you're aware of who you are, what you think, the way you behave and the impact you have, there's absolutely no way of making conscious decisions about it. The behaviour that you keep throwing out will keep coming back at you, and you'll wonder why you're never called back to the second interview, why you're always the one being hoicked in to have discussions with your manager about yet another comment that offended yet another colleague, why your job is always being restructured, why your team has the highest turnover rate and why your organisation can never retain its executives.

There are two defining moments on my journey that led me here.

The first was when I was working closely with four levels of people: the Road Blocks. Let's call them Steep Gradient, Emergency Stop, Uneven Camber and Slippery Surface. At one time or another, Steep Gradient, Emergency Stop and Uneven Camber had each been my line manager. Slippery Surface was managed by Emergency Stop and somehow had become increasingly involved in my area of work.

The project I led was new, not without complication, involved lots of partners and stakeholders and required a lot of attention to the financial details. I dreaded the steering group. It seemed to be an opportunity to review my work and berate me for not having achieved all the things on the action plan, regardless of whether delivery of the actions sat with me or not. It functioned more like a 15-person performance review.

One day, there had been a lot of conversations going back and forth between senior people and others responsible for delivering the project. I decided to ring Emergency Stop, as my manager, to debrief about what had gone on and think about next steps. Instead, Slippery Surface answered the phone. I received a tirade of abuse, and at one point they actually said that Emergency Stop was standing behind them and wanted the message conveyed to me that they were "sick of the project and didn't want to hear any more about it today". The verbal violence continued, and it was the one and only time in my professional career when I've had to tell another colleague that I was putting the phone down on them. This was how it went on. And on.

There was another occasion when, due to having had a seizure unexpectedly, I wasn't able to drive my car for a year. There was a government scheme that would pay for a taxi to take me to and from work. *Amazing*, I thought. I went to Steep Gradient, my manager at the time, and explained the situation, saying that the taxi times would have to be fixed because, you know, other people have lives and jobs to do… I said the taxi would drop me off at 8:30am and pick me up at 4:30am, meaning there may be the odd meeting I would have to leave early or promptly. Their response was to say that leaving things early probably wouldn't look good for me. If only I knew then what I know now about disability discrimination. Steep Gradient also caused a constructive dismissal case to be fought and lost by the organisation. Steep Gradient came from the old school of management where people did what you told them and work was in service to the boss. They were a bully, plain and simple.

Between them, they had displayed an array of unsavoury behaviours: disability discrimination, management by fear, bullying, a lack of emotional intelligence, disrespect, incivility and standing by when their direct report was being thrown under the bus, if not actually being the one doing the throwing. It took me a long time to recover from having worked in their midst, and I reflected long and hard about my experiences over many years.

The second was when I was working in a different organisation, and I came across an individual who was a leader. They didn't have 'leader' in their job title; they didn't have 'manager' or 'supervisor' in their job title – in fact, they didn't line manage anyone at all. But they led. And they shall henceforth be called the Fairy Goth Mother. They were able to represent the voices of their colleagues, translating the worries of the many into a conversation with the few. They had the ability to act as a go-between and translate worker worries into management speak and translate manager speak into "What they're really trying to say is…" They had the type of understated authority and reputational gravitas that made them a trusted colleague to all levels of the team. They weren't afraid to bring matters to the attention of senior colleagues, and they didn't shy away from having reality-check conversations with peers who wanted the moon on a stick and the removal of tasks from their job description with a pay rise.

I kept coming back to these two different experiences and these five different people and tried to figure out what it was about them and the situations I'd experienced that kept me replaying the stories in my head. And I replayed them for years and years.

During those years, I'd explored doing a PhD. There was one particular course I wanted to do – a taught Doctor of Business Administration (DBA) at the University of South Wales (USW). Unfortunately, the bursary opportunities had ended, so I looked around at two or three different universities. Every single one I talked to told me how difficult a doctorate would be, and I came away thinking that I just wasn't up to it. Then, in 2016, I saw a 'Certificate of Governance' course on offer at USW. It turned out the course wouldn't be running that year because there hadn't been enough interest. I asked about the DBA again to be told there was a new course director who'd changed the application and fee structure, and within the space of two weeks, I was on the course. If something's meant for you, it won't go by you, so they say!

In thinking about my topic, I wanted it to be something that would keep me interested after five years of study. I decided I wanted to focus on something that involved people watching, which brought me back to my two experiences. So, what was it about these two experiences? What connected them?

I considered what the individuals might have thought of me and their own behaviours, what others thought of them. I thought about what the organisations' senior executives knew about them and whether they just let it go or simply had no idea. The connections between the experiences took shape, and I discovered they were the behaviours of people in the workplace towards others, behaviours of people at different levels, behaviours of people with leadership titles and those without, relationships and interactions and, here's the clincher, were any of these people aware of the impact they had on others?

That's how it all started.

The first experience made me unwell, sad, upset, knocked my confidence, rubbished my self-esteem and taught me loads. I'm glad I was able to come through it with the support of colleagues. I went to work somewhere else, a place that taught me about respect, the benefits of working together, camaraderie, collegiality, friendship, community and care. All those things allowed me to grow and heal to the point where I could look back and reflect on my experiences more objectively and draw learning from them.

I look back now and, to the Road Blocks, I say, "Thanks for my doctorate. I deserved it!" To the Fairy Goth Mother, I say, "I'm so grateful for people like you!"

The Green, Green Grass of Home[1]

Throughout this book, I refer to Wales. Wales is the country between England and Ireland and is one of the four countries that make up the UK. Lots of people who aren't from the UK have never heard of it or, if they have, don't know that it's not a part of England. Actually, that the whole of the UK isn't England!

Wales is my home. I was born and bred there, and for the first 20 or so years of my working life, I spent it there. I grew up on the west coast, closer to Ireland than England, and I moved east to university. I lived in and near Cardiff and the South Wales Valleys for the following 20 years. My Welsh working life was spent in the public sector, between the National Health Service and local government. It was a natural progression for me to do my doctoral research focussed on the Welsh public service. It was what I knew and it was what I loved.

In 2019, I'd been working in my organisation for nearly eight years and decided I should look for the next career move whilst I still loved my job. I didn't want to hang around until I hated it and get to the point where I was scrabbling to get out. A restructure was announced and I was offered redundancy. I was overwhelmed with excitement at the potential to do something different. I spent a long time looking at job sites and reading adverts but couldn't find anything that quite hit the spot. The public-sector financial climate in Wales was such that senior people were staying put or, if they did leave, jobs were being deleted behind them. That meant my opportunities in Wales were limited to nil.

I said to my husband, "The only place I can find opportunities are in London. Shall we move to London?"

"Okay!" he said.

And so, we moved to London.

Working in England was a bit strange at first because the public-sector structures are different and they only operate in one language! Wales is a bilingual country – another thing people are surprised by. Yes, Welsh is a language and it's very much alive and well. All Welsh public bodies provide documentation in both Welsh and English, and services must have an 'active offer', where all citizens are asked if they want services through the medium of Welsh or English. Welsh-medium school attainment is very high, and waiting lists for Welsh-medium schools are getting longer.

This is why you'll hear me refer to Wales occasionally, and you will find the odd Welsh institution and place name referenced throughout the book.

Wales runs through me like a seam of gold. Welsh gold.

Cymru am byth!

The Research

In October 2016, I embarked on my DBA. The aim of my study was to critically explore self-awareness and its relevance to leader effectiveness across all levels of the Welsh public service.

The objectives were to 1) explore the concept of self-awareness within the workplace context of the Welsh public service, 2) examine the relationship between self-awareness and leader effectiveness in the Welsh public service and 3) determine whether self-aware leaders can be found at all job levels of the Welsh public service.

To achieve these objectives, I set out four research questions:

- Is there a relationship between self-awareness and resonant leader effectiveness?

- Will effective resonant leaders be identified at all five levels of Welsh public service organisations?

- Do effective resonant leaders within the strategic job level have greater self-awareness than effective leaders identified at any of the other four job levels of Welsh public service organisations?

- Do effective resonant leaders identified at all five levels of the Welsh public service have greater self-awareness than those who are identified as ineffective?

Through my research, I established a unique three-layer definition of self-awareness, which forms the basis of the definition of self-aware leadership I use throughout this book.

As part of my research, I carried out a literature review of academic papers and books and carried out a questionnaire followed by some interviews. From the questionnaire and interviews, I found there was a relationship between self-awareness and leader effectiveness. Effective resonant leaders could be identified at all five levels of the Welsh public service organisations. Effective resonant leaders at the strategic level had less self-awareness than those at any other level. Effective resonant leaders at the operational, business, management and senior management levels had greater self-awareness than those who were ineffective. Line managers identified as effective resonant leaders at the business, management and senior management job levels had greater self-awareness than those who were identified as ineffective.

The qualitative data yielded a number of areas for consideration, such as behaviour, organisational standards, the experiences of individuals, strategic-level disconnect and reflection. Other themes, like people management, the potential of individuals, community connections and impact of decisions, were also highlighted as relevant. Discussion topics such as inclusive decision making, co-operation between peers and recruitment processes emerged too. You'll see these themes and topics throughout the book.

I concluded my thesis by making five recommendations for improvement:

1. strategic review of organisational culture to raise the profile of relational skills;

2. refocus of organisational priorities in people management, communication and recruitment-marketing strategies, policies and procedures to align with organisational culture;

3. review of recruitment, retention, capability management, training and organisational development policies and procedures to align with organisational culture and priorities;

4. assessment of individual self-awareness through recruitment and promotion processes;

5. operationalisation of organisational standards.

As you read through the nine CHARTABLE compass points, the signposts and directions, and roadblocks and trip hazards, you'll see these recommendations knitted through the narrative.

Knowing Self Knowing Others: Blog and Podcast

My website, ksko.co.uk, went live in 2018. I started dabbling in writing about my research as a way of giving life to what I was learning. But it wasn't until 2020 that my website really started living!

I completed my final doctoral thesis in May 2020, but because of Covid and going back and forth with my uni supervisors, the oral exam didn't land in my diary until March 2021. I started to worry that the huge gap between May and March would mean I'd forget a lot of what I'd learnt. I was also conscious that I'd never really talked to people about my research, because I was doing it outside of work – it wasn't really related to what I did, even if it did inform the way I did it. I'd never had to formulate the phrases about self-aware leadership out loud with anyone other than my supervisors, which made me feel at a disadvantage when going into an oral exam. I decided to start blogging about my research, using language that made the subject interesting and accessible to people in the world of work. I did this on my website and on LinkedIn, and it attracted a lot of interest and positive feedback.

My oral exam went well, and I passed my doctorate with minor amendments, which means they ask you to make some minor changes to your thesis and resubmit it. Only if things have gone seriously out of whack would you fail at this point!!

I'd always wanted to make my thesis into a book: something useful, like a practical guide to improvement. Over a year after my oral exam, I still hadn't written my book. I realised that unless I did something more visible and dynamic, all the hard work I'd put into my studies would end up sitting on the shelf in my big green hardbound 90,000-word thesis, collecting dust. So, I started a podcast in September 2022: *The Knowing Self Knowing Others Podcast.*

I discuss self-aware leadership with thinkers from around the globe, and it's available on all your favourite podcast platforms. It's an interview-based podcast, and for the first year, I posed the same five questions to all my guests:

- How do you define self-awareness?
- What are your thoughts on the relationship between self-awareness and leader effectiveness?
- Do you think effective leaders can be found at all levels, and why?
- Do you think leaders at the most strategic level of organisations have greater self-awareness than leaders at other levels of organisations? What experiences have informed your view?
- What do you think is an effective way to develop self-awareness?

The questions were modified versions of the interview questions I'd used in my research and were designed to grow that body of evidence.

During the second year, I decided to make the questions more fluid and less tightly constrained to my stock research questions but still very much about the exploration and promotion of self-aware leadership across the globe.

After every episode, I do a top takeaways review of the discussion I've had with my guest. These top takeaways feature throughout this book and balance my academic research with research into what's really happening on the ground.

How to Read This Book

This book is set out in parts, chapters and sections. It has three parts, nine chapters and many sections.

Each chapter begins with a 'chapter map' of your upcoming reading journey to introduce you to the chapter ahead and summarise what twists and turns are coming up. Every chapter ends with a look in 'the rear-view mirror' to reflect on the important things for you to take away, think about, remember, share and use on your self-awareness journey.

Part 1 – Why are you here, traveller? This part sets out the 'why' of this guidebook. It's all about defining and describing self-awareness, leader effectiveness, leadership at all levels and why all these things are important to you. It's made up of three chapters and will take you on a journey of discovery through my three-layer definition of self-awareness, the connection between self-awareness and emotional intelligence, the differences between men and women, introverts and extroverts, and hard and relational skills. You'll also explore the nature–nurture debate, find out what the five levels of organisations are, and the differences between leaders with titles and leaders without. At the end of Part 1, we'll put it all together to describe self-aware leadership in one clear, combined definition.

Part 2 – Where are you going? This part is all about the 'where' of this guidebook, and it has three chapters. Even though self-awareness is not a destination, you still have choices in the roads you travel, the decisions you make and the values you hold dear whilst you journey between entering this world and exiting it. The first chapter presents my unique and important gift to you: a self-awareness compass. It has nine direction points to help you chart your journey along your superhighway, derived from my research findings and discoveries. They are the CHARTABLE compass points of care, humility, authenticity, reflection, trust, adaptability, behaviour, listening and experience. It will then describe signposts and directions to help you on your journey, such as strategy, organisational standards, people management, wellbeing, teamwork and inclusive decision making. It will also give you a heads-up on roadblocks and trip hazards – like disconnection, red tape, stress, toxicity and accidental leadership – that will create obstacles and barriers along your journey. At the end of Part 2, you'll have an understanding of all the things you need to consider to ensure your journey on your Self-Awareness Superhighway is purposeful, positive and fulfilling.

Part 3 – How will you get there? The third and final part of the book takes you on a quest of 'how'. It will share some tools and techniques to help you develop your self-aware leadership through reflection, recognition and regulation. It will explore mindfulness, psychometric tests and assessment tools, journaling, coaching, trusted feedback and 360-degree reviews. It will also explain the unique Compass Quiz that's been developed especially for you as part of this book. It's a very specific tool to take your learning from this book into action. The quiz will give you an opportunity to discover which of the compass directions you should be travelling in, helping you develop your self-aware leadership skills through an assessment carried out by you and an assessment carried out by others.

Chapter 9 is the arrivals lounge of the book. As with every entry to an arrivals lounge, it signals the end of one leg of a journey and the beginning of another. Chapter 9 will be the end of my time travelling with you and a reflection of our whole journey together. It will look back at what you have learnt, the journey you have travelled and consider where you want to go next on your Self-Awareness Superhighway.

I hope you enjoy your learning journey and, along the way, feel inspired to do more, do different and do better, to benefit yourself and others. I hope you try out some new techniques and find the ones that suit you best. I hope you talk about relationships and self-awareness with your colleagues and promote a culture of greater self-aware leadership in your organisations so that, together, we generate kinder, more respectful and creative working relationships through reflection, recognition and regulation.

PART 1
WHY ARE YOU HERE, TRAVELLER?

2. WHAT IS SELF-AWARENESS?

Chapter Map

Welcome to the first chapter of the first part. Please bring your seat to the upright position, ready for take-off.

Come with me on your self-awareness journey of discovery. You'll explore the long history of the concept of self-awareness and how we've arrived at today, knowing what we know. You'll investigate my definition of self-awareness. It might be a little different to what you've heard before because it has three layers instead of two. Then we'll discuss the great debate about self-awareness and emotional intelligence. Is self-awareness an element of emotional intelligence, or is emotional intelligence an element of self-awareness? We'll explore the differences between the self-awareness of men and women in the world of work, and finally you'll find out more about differences between introverts and extroverts. We'll round up by considering why all of this is important and why you are here!

Onward, traveller!

The Journey of Self-Awareness

If I asked you, "What is self-awareness?", what would you say?

For the first year of my podcast, I asked every single guest the question: "How do you define self-awareness?" It seemed to make sense to start the conversation by making sure we were talking about the same thing. Jacqui Frost (episode 9), a leadership coach with a background as a headteacher and schools advisor, said that, on the face of it, self-awareness is a simple concept until you start talking about it and exploring it. Then you realise it is like unpeeling an onion and discovering that there's another layer to be explored, and another.

Lots of my guests have said, "It's know yourself". However, they've gone on to say that when they've really thought about it (and to give something more interesting than a three-word answer!), it's actually far more complicated than that. And so, starting this book by defining it is really important because there's far more to the little phrase 'know yourself' than first meets the eye.

Let me begin by first going backwards. Sometimes you have to reverse to get yourself in just the right position to go forward; otherwise, you'll forever be a little off-course.

We've been trying to understand ourselves for thousands of years. This thirst for self-awareness is nothing new. The ancient Greek aphorism 'know thyself', one of the bedrocks of the concept of self-awareness, is associated with Aristotle, Socrates and great thinkers from thousands of years ago. Socrates said that to know yourself, you've got to see yourself as if you're looking through the eyes of someone else.

"I seem to be wiser than this man in so far as I do not think I know what I do not know. I recognise myself... as knowing nothing." [1]

If you type 'know thyself' into Wikipedia, there's a really good explanation of where the phrase comes from and photos of where it's etched into the stone at the Temple of Apollo at Delphi. With a mind as complicated as a human's, and being that emotions are the things that set us apart from artificial intelligence, I'm sure 'know thyself' will continue to be one of the greatest quests of humankind long into the 21st century.

This whole idea of self-knowledge and 'knowing what I know I know' is called metaknowledge,[2] or meta-cognitive ability.[3] It's described as "knowing when to see a doctor or a lawyer" rather than "how much you know about medicine and law".[4] This descriptor separates out *what* you do from *how* you do it. As you continue reading, you'll notice that *what* (doing) and *how* (thinking) are often used to help describe things in this book. 'What you do' is called primary or first-order knowledge, and 'how you do things' is called secondary or second-order knowledge – and we'll talk more about these two things later.

When you read about self-awareness, people tend to describe it in two parts: internal self-awareness and external self-awareness, or social self-awareness. I'll start by describing these two layers because they're the foundation of my three-layer definition. Then I'll go on to explain why I see self-awareness as actually being made up of three parts.

As it's journeyed through time, internal self-awareness has been called many different things by many different people. The first time I spotted it in literature was in a paper from 1975, where it was being called 'private self-consciousness'.[5] Then, in 2001, it was referred to as 'objective self-awareness'[6] and in 2002, 'intrapersonal intelligence'.[7] Every description had a slightly different slant to it. In 2014, the term 'internal self-awareness' was first used when it was described as an ability to get in touch with and learn about one's "characters, traits, beliefs, values, strengths, abilities, motivations and desires" and "an understanding of how one thinks and feel in different situations".[8] I decided to stick with the term 'internal self-awareness' because it was the most recent one I could find.

When you explore internal self-awareness, you get into really deep, existential questions about the 'self'. It feels a bit like quantum physics of the soul. Blows your mind a bit! Before you can get to a position of being able to talk about your own internal self-awareness and social self-awareness, you've first got to have an appreciation that you are a 'self'. You need to understand that you are a sentient being who has thoughts, feelings and opinions. You're a human-*being* first and foremost, who lives, loves and journeys through life 'in relation' to other people, rather than a human-*doing*, who's just reacting to external stimuli on a subconscious level. Executive coach Dr Gerrit Pelzer (episode 22) talked to me about this on my podcast. He said there is no one agreed-upon definition of self-awareness or self. There is no identified part of the brain that is the source of the self. Self is just your response to your internal and external world, which is always changing. The self is a perception, not a fact. You create it from the stories you tell yourself and others tell you.

Gerrit also said the idea of the isolated self is an illusion because we're all connected – the air you breathe is impacted by the plants around you, plants create the food you consume, your food impacts your gut bacteria, which impacts how you feel, and on and on the connections go. Katrijn van Oudheusden (episode 26), a coach, trainer and author, also talked about connectedness and the philosophy of non-duality, which is a way of thinking about the self as interconnected, not separate, which comes from Eastern philosophy, particularly Taoism. There are different ways of thinking about the self: the psychological self, which considers us as people who make choices about our directions and our interactions, and the essential self, which considers us as entities that are interconnected and move with the flow of the world around us.

This idea of the 'self reflecting on the self' always brings up this question about how can you ever be sufficiently objective to accurately reflect on yourself? Well, maybe this is *the thing*. You're not! What you're trying to do, day in and day out on the journey of self-awareness, is to widen this gap between the subjective self, which never accepts you can ever be wrong about anything, and the objective self, which has enough awareness to go, "Oh shit, I messed up." There's a great line in Stephen Shedletzky's book, *Speak-Up Culture*: "It's very hard to read the label on the jar when you're stuck inside the jar." This is exactly the challenge you have every day – trying to get a peek at the labels on the outside of your jar!

And then, of course, you change. Your 'self' is an ongoing narrative, rather than a static constant, that experiences change, reversal and surprise, which in turn creates a changing and evolving self. Change is the only constant, and even if it's just that you age, get stiffer and a little greyer, change is inevitable! That means the way you describe yourself and the definition you hold of yourself changes depending on the situation and any external influences at any given point in time. When you think about your interactions with others and your constant shift in who you know, who you spend time with and who you work with, none of it ever stays the same, ergo changing self, changing others: knowing self, knowing others!

My podcast guests have shared this same idea many times over. When I spoke to the co-founder of The Happiness Index, Matthew Phelan (episode 13), he was clear that your definition of self changes over time and that we're all on a journey of getting to know our strengths, weaknesses and impact on others. We're different people than we were yesterday. We'll have had life-changing events, like births, deaths and marriages, and they'll all have influenced how we see the world, see ourselves and interact with other people. Assistant fire chief of the city of Petaluma Chad Costa (episode 23) said the same. Former British Army captain Liam Maguire (episode 19), a director of people and operations, introduced me to a quote I just love by Robert Breault, "Know thyself, or at least keep renewing the acquaintance." Exactly. Knowing yourself isn't a destination; it's a journey, and you need to keep reflecting on where you've come from, where you are and where you're going. Síle Walsh (episode 14), inclusive leadership, organisational development and coaching psychology expert, said you shouldn't be mistaken that finding out a little bit about yourself means you know everything about yourself!! Your little bit of self-awareness has simply reduced the size of your blind spot for a little while. You haven't erased it altogether!

When I did my research interviews, a number of interviewees shared their own thoughts about the definition of self-awareness. They said things like, "Self-awareness is multi-faceted. It's understanding your own needs, others' needs, impact of self on others, impact of others on self." They also talked about what self-awareness wasn't, and that's been a clear theme throughout my research and podcasting too. People define things in terms of what they are and what they are not. This is helpful in giving descriptors 'outlines': you know what's inside the lines, and you know what's outside.

When you think about the self-awareness of a leader, a major component of the relationship between a leader and followers is how the leader sees or perceives themself. How you see yourself impacts how you react to others, which impacts how they react to you. You can't think of self-awareness without thinking of an exchange and reciprocity. This takes you nicely on to the idea, even if just for a minute, of what happens when the view you have of yourself is incongruous with the views that other people have of you.

When you've got a senior exec who thinks they're kind and generous but all the people around them think they're boastful and arrogant, what does this mean for working relationships? What does this mean for organisational success? This is what the 'self/other ratings studies' are all about. We'll talk more about them later, but simply, these studies show that how you rate your performance and leadership is often inflated when your self-awareness is low. People who over-rate themselves are often poor performers.[9]

How then do you put all of this together to define internal self-awareness? Well, my definition of internal self-awareness is...

An ability to recognise the self's changing thoughts, feelings, beliefs, values, strengths and abilities through reflection and introspection.

Now, that's all fine and dandy when I'm presenting my doctoral thesis to university examiners, but what does that mean to you in your everyday working life? Well, it's simply **reflection**. Internal self-awareness is the act and art of reflecting inwards on your own thoughts, feelings, beliefs, values, strengths and abilities.

The other part of self-awareness you'll most commonly hear referenced is social self-awareness, or external self-awareness. It's changed and morphed over time, in name and description, just like internal self-awareness. It's had different names like 'public self-consciousness',[10] 'subjective self-awareness',[11] 'interpersonal intelligence'[12] and 'social side of self-awareness'.[13] I call it social self-awareness, which is a slightly more catchy version of the most recent incarnation of the name I could find.

Social self-awareness is all about the awareness of self in relation to others: the part of self-awareness that considers interactions with others. It encompasses everything you do, say and are in relation to others. It takes the introspection part of self-awareness, which is all about just you, and adds that next dimension to it – the *outrospection* of yourself, which includes other people (yes, it's a word – I checked).

For me, internal self-awareness and social self-awareness fit together like layers of an onion, just like Jacqui Frost (episode 9) said! You can't be truly socially self-aware unless you are first internally self-aware.

Here's a model of what we know about self-awareness so far:

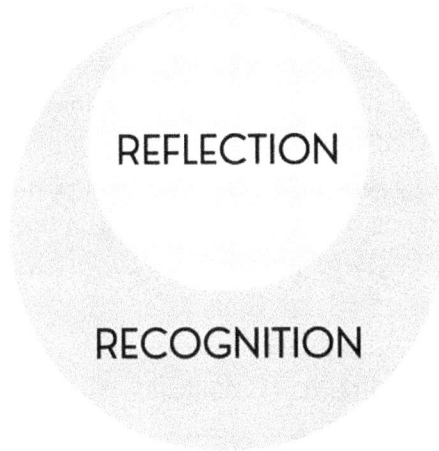

REFLECTION

RECOGNITION

A Different Definition of Self-Awareness

Now that we've talked about internal and social self-awareness, I can tell you about my slightly different take on it. In the descriptions of social self-awareness, there appear to be elements of introspection as well as elements of outrospection. It's not all about what's going on 'out there'. In a 2014 study by Showry and Manasa,[14] they talk about "an ability to see how others view the self", which is a step away from internal self-awareness, but it's not quite all the way over there to the furthest point of social self-awareness. I developed this idea of internal-social self-awareness, which is the overlapping part of a relationship between you and someone else. It's that point where your interactions collide, where you notice each other, perceive each other and usually make judgement calls about each other.

My academic definition is...

**An ability to recognise how the self is received by,
perceived by and impacts others.**

The way I describe it in the everyday is to call it **recognition**.

I often present to large groups of people; sometimes they're people I know and sometimes they're complete strangers. Some will be listening intently, some will be taking notes, some will be chatting to the person next to them, some will be scrolling on their phones. This is recognition: their response to my behaviour and my recognition of their response. I've spotted the behaviours of the note-takers and the phone-scrollers, and in recognising these behaviours, I can dip into my self-awareness toolkit and choose to regulate my behaviour to elicit a different response from the audience.

The third layer of my definition of self-awareness is external-social self-awareness. It's the outer layer of social self-awareness.

If there are more phone-scrollers than note-takers in the audience, I need to do something about the impact I'm having on them. I can do that through changing my behaviour. I start speaking faster, I leave a pause to get people's attention, I throw in a few jokes, I pose some questions to the floor. Now, I'm reflecting on the change I've just made in my behaviour, recognising that the phone-scrollers have lifted their heads, and I'm deciding to continue to regulate my behaviour and be more dynamic and interactive in my presentation. That's self-awareness in the moment and an example of a common type of relationship you have with other people.

'Social intelligence' has lots of similarities to the third layer of self-awareness. It's described as "the ability to think and act wisely in social situations".[15] It's also described as "the ability to express oneself in social interactions, the ability to 'read' and understand different social situations, knowledge of social roles, norms, and scripts, interpersonal problem-solving skills, and social role-playing skills".[16] All these things allow a leader to manage social exchanges and display appropriate adult emotional responses (whatever they are!) in social interactions.[17]

My definition of external-social self-awareness is:

An ability to read and understand the emotions and intentions of others and respond and act wisely in social exchanges.

And I affectionately refer to it as **regulation**.

When I spoke to Matt Stone (episode 10), CEO of BehavioralOS, his view was that self-awareness gives you choices. When you come to better understand your range of behaviour, you give yourself a range of choices in how you want to behave in a given situation – so you get to respond, not react. Think back to the example above – speeding up, pausing, humour and audience participation were some choices I had. This is exactly what the regulation layer is about. Getting to choose from a place of awareness. Matt said that relationships are dynamic and we're always moving closer or moving further apart from each other. We're never in stasis. He said we're all squishy and complicated; we come with our own flavour and dance to different tunes. When you pay attention to how you dance and others dance, you have a choice of how you want to dance with them. To tango or not to tango? That is the question!

This is my definition of self-awareness, and it's the three-layer definition of self-awareness that I'll use throughout this book. When I refer to self-awareness, I'm talking about all three layers:

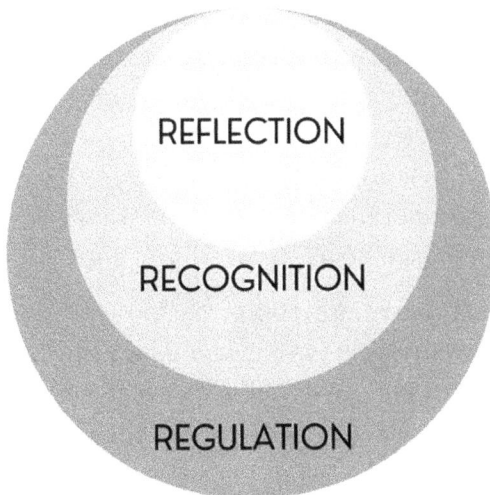

REFLECTION

RECOGNITION

REGULATION

The Self/Other Ratings Studies

The self/other ratings studies are the foundational pieces of literature related to self-awareness and how it plays out in practice. They're important because what I've found on my learning journey is a little different to what the self/other ratings studies discovered.

Jump into my taxi and let me take you on a trip...

The self/other ratings studies make up a large section of the literature about self-awareness.[18] Their basic methodological premise is 'I rate me, you rate me.' If you know anything about 360-degree reviews, you'll understand this kind of assessment idea and process. The studies present the incongruity[19] between the viewpoints of the self and the viewpoints of others and the implication this has on relationships.[20] The studies generally focus on individuals who hold senior positions in organisations. Hold on to this thought because it becomes relevant to the discoveries that you'll read about later.

The study that seems to be seminal is by Atwater and Yammarino, and the others generally corroborate the findings from this study:

- Self-ratings tend to be inflated, meaning 'I think I'm more capable than I really am.'

- Self-ratings are less highly related to ratings by others than others' ratings are with each other, meaning when you consider 'my ratings of me' versus 'other people's ratings of me', other people generally have a more consistent view between themselves than I do with them. If you think about this from a 360-degree review perspective, what this means is that of those five people who rated you, all five are likely to have similar views. Your view in comparison to what the five of them think may be similar or poles apart, depending on how self-aware you are.

- Inaccurate self-raters are poorer performers than accurate self-raters, meaning people who give inflated self-ratings and those people who are poles apart in their view of themselves compared to other people's view of them tend to be poorer performers.

**"Those who are more aware of how they're perceived by others...
are rated as more transformational by their subordinates; and these
leaders are the best performers."[21]**

The Dunning-Kruger effect[22] describes this over-raters problem best.
Dunning and Kruger discovered that a lack of ability not only causes poor
performance but also the inability to recognise that performance is poor.
Oh, the irony. The "bottom quartile of individuals on a test of logical
reasoning scored on average at the 12th percentile whilst they estimated
their score at the 62nd percentile".[23] Eeeek!

In *Think Again* by Adam Grant, I was awestruck to discover that Adam
went to university with David Dunning and Justin Kruger (not that Adam
Grant isn't impressive in his own right). He dedicates a whole section to
the Dunning-Kruger effect and over-estimation of abilities:

**"[Dunning and Kruger] found that in many situations, those who
can't... don't know they can't. According to what's now known as the
Dunning-Kruger effect, it's when you lack competence that you're
most likely to be brimming with overconfidence... The less intelligent
you are in a particular domain, the more you seem to overestimate
your actual intelligence in that domain."**

'Empty vessels make the most noise' is how I usually describe the
Dunning-Kruger effect. In contrast, under-raters of self-awareness are
rated as having the highest self-awareness by direct reports[24] because
underestimation in a self-rating is linked to greater self-awareness,
modesty and humility.[25] This connects us to Socrates' idea that the more
you know, the more you realise just how little you know!

People I interviewed during my research gave a number of examples
of the benefits of being self-aware. They said it gave them an opportunity
to question and reflect on their approach before acting. They talked
about the ability to pause and decide rather than jumping in with knee-
jerk reactions without thinking them through first. One interviewee said
that some people without self-awareness were initially seen as 'doers'
but then they stagnated. They could pull off the initial 'wow' but couldn't
bring people along the change journey with them and, being that they

weren't reflective enough to change, they became less relevant to the long game. A bit of a one-trick pony. They said that, with awareness of position power, leaders could really influence change and make a difference.

The Self-Awareness vs Emotional Intelligence Debate

You'll have probably come across emotional intelligence more often than self-awareness as a topic of workplace and leadership discussion. I too had heard more about emotional intelligence than self-awareness when I started on this learning journey. The interconnectivity, overlap and interchange between emotional intelligence and self-awareness is very evident in the academic journals. Self-awareness seems bigger than emotional intelligence, though. After all, self-awareness is awareness of your whole self – your hair, your shoes, your car, your eye rolls... the whole thing! Career and life coach Sophie Bryan (episode 17) said that self-awareness is introspection of the heart, mind, soul and body: it's a whole-body experience.

Daniel Goleman is generally viewed as the guru of emotional intelligence, even though it was first discussed by Salovey and Mayer (1990),[26] Goleman says self-awareness is a facet of emotional intelligence. His definition of emotional intelligence started life in 1995 with four pillars: self-awareness, self-management, social awareness and relationship management. A fifth pillar, motivation, was added in 1998. The original four pillars definitely have alignment with the three-layer definition of self-awareness I use in this book. But when you read what Goleman says about self-awareness, his description seems to align with just internal self-awareness.

Three of the self/other ratings studies[27] focus on emotional intelligence rather than self-awareness. They conceptualise emotional intelligence as self-awareness and hold the view that emotional intelligence is the same as self-awareness.[28] Because of the difficulties of establishing the presence of emotional intelligence, a viable alternative to doing so is to use findings from studies that explore the view of the self held by the self and the view of the self held by others.[29] Together, the studies show that emotional intelligence and self-awareness are inextricable, if not interchangeable in some contexts. In this book, self-awareness is defined as being greater than emotional intelligence and emotional intelligence is a part of self-awareness, but the two things are very closely connected, and sometimes they'll be referred to together.

The Women vs Men Debate

One of the greatest public examples of self-awareness has come from Jacinda Ardern, Prime Minister of New Zealand from 2017 to 2023. She guided New Zealand through Covid with humility and a people-centric approach. She was held up as an exemplar of good leadership. When she resigned, she used the words "I no longer have enough in the tank": an insightful comment demonstrating her awareness of her dwindling energy reserves and being on a road to burnout. In her resignation speech, she said:

"Now, I cannot determine what will define my time in this place, but I do hope I've demonstrated something else entirely: that you can be anxious, sensitive, kind, and wear your heart on your sleeve, you can be a mother or not, you can be an ex-Mormon or not, you can be a nerd, a crier, a hugger—you can be all of these things, and not only can you be here; you can lead. Just like me."[30]

Two of the self/other ratings studies[31] considered the impact of gender on self-awareness. They found that "direct reports rated women significantly higher on self-awareness than they rated men. Whilst women managers do not perceive themselves as more self-aware than their male counterparts, they're perceived as such by people who report to them."[32]

Some of my research interviewees said they felt there was a burgeoning change, with a high number of female managers coming up the career ladder and working alongside older male managers, which created interesting relationships. This is reflected in a report produced by the Equality and Human Rights Commission in 2017, *Who runs Wales?*,[33] which said, "While women make up the majority of the public-sector workforce in Wales, this is not generally reflected in positions of power. Two sectors (health and education) made considerable progress, showing that it can be done." I suspect that's a pretty accurate statement for most Western countries.

An article in *Forbes*, 'New Research: Women More Effective Than Men In All Leadership Measures', paints a very clear picture of the behavioural advantages women have in being able to lead effectively. Some of my top takeaways from the article are...

- Women leaders score significantly higher in their capabilities to connect and relate to others and are better at building relationships characterised by authenticity and awareness of how they contribute to the greater good beyond the leaders' immediate sphere of influence.

- Women are more likely to lead from a creative mindset and 'play for all to win'.

- Women build and cultivate stronger connections – building caring connections, mentoring and developing others, and exhibiting concern for the community.

- Female leaders demonstrate higher levels of leadership effectiveness and creative competencies, and they demonstrate lower reactive impact compared to their male counterparts.

When I spoke to Kyle McDowell (episode 32), author of *Begin With WE*, he said that, in his experience, he'd found women typically more self-aware than men. Our conversation went on to consider whether the connection between the concepts of self-awareness, vulnerability and leadership acted as barriers to men showing greater emotion in the world of work and whether building psychological safety around men would be a good thing for everybody.

Take a reflective pause for a moment and think about the people in your workplace. What are your thoughts on the level of self-awareness amongst your colleagues? Do you think there's a gender-related pattern?

Introverts vs Extroverts

Self-awareness is different for introverts and extroverts. You might be someone who knows instantly whether you're an introvert or an extrovert, or maybe you're an ambivert or omnivert. Wherever your strengths lie, self-awareness will be different for you compared to someone else.

I've been lucky to share a microphone with Joanna Rawbone, Megumi Miki and Serena Low, all of whom are active promoters and staunch advocates of the skills, strengths and power of introverts and quieter people. Joanna Rawbone (episode 6), founder of Flourishing Introverts, very helpfully described the way extroverts operate as 'talk-think-talk' and introverts as 'think-talk-think', which is one of the best descriptors I've ever heard. The internal monologue that generates the reflection for an introvert happens before they speak. For an extrovert, they speak first and reflect later. Introverts draw their energy from introspection, whilst extroverts draw their energy from outrospection. Introverts and extroverts are at different starting points in their self-reflection journeys and self-awareness development. If reflection is your normal modus operandi, it's going to be easier for you to go there. If it's not, then it's not.

My conversation with Joanna Rawbone is the second most popular episode since the podcast was launched in September 2022. Joanna described the 'extraversion bias' that exists both in the social and professional world. She said we are surrounded by an unspoken understanding that those out at the front shouting loudest are better than those sitting quietly at the back. We ask, what's the problem with the employee who doesn't speak in meetings? The quieter ones are told to speak up more… Have you been asked to speak up more? Have you been the one doing the asking?

I used to work with an out-and-out extrovert – let's call them Sonic Boom. I remember a particularly squirmy conversation I spectated. We were in a meeting with another colleague; let's call her Mrs Pointer. Thankfully, it was just the three of us. Mrs Pointer's husband was also employed in the organisation, in quite a senior position. Sonic proceeded to tell Mrs Pointer that they'd met her husband recently for the first time and had been surprised at how much smaller he was than they'd expected, given that he was in a senior position and all. Without a breath, they continued down this slippery slope, saying they'd imagined him to be taller and more imposing given his level of seniority. At this point, Mrs Pointer had to step in and defend her husband with something like, "Oh, you don't want to cross him. You don't want to be on the wrong side of him when he's angry, etc., etc."... Sonic rarely did anything to endear themself to anyone, so part of me enjoyed the show and wondered just how deep they'd dig the hole. Another part of me just wanted to melt into the furniture. Sonic never made any reference to the conversation nor suggested they had any realisation of the grave disrespect they'd just shown to someone's husband and a senior officer of the organisation to boot. I'm pretty sure Mrs Pointer will have remembered and logged it for future use.

Megumi Miki (episode 31), leadership consultant and author of the highly acclaimed *Quietly Powerful*, describes quietly powerful leaders as understated, humble and good listeners. She says they are present, comfortable in their own skin and have the confidence to be vulnerable. They empower others and encourage other people to shine because they don't need the attention and limelight themselves. They're often people who don't say much, but when they do speak, they make a big impact. These leaders are aware of their style and consciously use it as a leadership strength. Megumi believes that not-so-quiet leaders have a lot to learn from these quietly powerful leaders. Jon Rennie (episode 11), business leader and host of the *Deep Leadership* podcast, said a lot of great answers come from the quieter voices. Leaders need to create opportunities for introverts to share their ideas and have their voices heard. Organisational leaders tend to pass by the introverts who are sitting and thinking silently whilst the extroverts are taking up the airspace. He said that you need to listen to the quieter voices because, sometimes, they're the ones with the best ideas.

I listened to the *Soft Skills for Leaders* podcast hosted by Lisa Evans in discussion with Serena Low, who is an introvert coach focussing on emotional intelligence, empathy and trauma-informed coaching and hosts *The Quiet Warrior Podcast*. I was so interested in what Serena said about introversion that I called her up. We talked about reflection and how introverts have a head start when it comes to the journey of self-awareness. Reflection is one of the key behaviours necessary for leader effectiveness (and we'll talk more about it later). If introverts are reflecting in steps one and three (think-talk-think) and extroverts are reflecting in step two (talk-think-talk), then introverts are off the starting blocks before the extroverts, and they're doing it for 66% of the time compared to 33% for extroverts. That means it's a behaviour that extroverts have to work harder at than introverts.

Does this mean introverts are more effective self-aware leaders than extroverts? No. What it means is that different people consider and contribute differently and make decisions differently. What I'd like you to take away from this section is that quiet doesn't necessarily mean incapable, and loud doesn't necessarily mean capable. As a self-aware leader, ensure your skills in the behaviours of care, humility, reflection and listening are attuned to all of the different types of people in your organisation. Don't let the noise drown out the quiet answers.

In the Rear-View Mirror

You've completed the first leg of your journey, and you've earned a little pit stop to eat some sandwiches, drink a flask of tea and look in your rear-view mirror to see where you've been.

You have a clear understanding of what self-awareness means in this book, and you know that self-awareness might not be as easy to define as simply 'know yourself'. You've gone back through the history of self-awareness and discovered 'know thyself' as a founding phrase of description. You've considered the implications of life events and how they change you and your self-awareness. You've walked through the definition of self-awareness, from internal self-awareness to internal-social self-awareness to external-social self-awareness. From here on in, these three layers will be known as the reflection, recognition and regulation layers. You've also heard about the self/other ratings studies and the founding body of research they generated about self-awareness, describing both what it is and what it isn't. You've discovered the Dunning-Kruger effect, which is both fascinating and ironically funny, and confirmed that the phrase 'empty vessels make the most noise' really is painfully accurate.

You've explored the similarities and differences between self-awareness and emotional intelligence and how many of the self/other ratings studies use the terms interchangeably. You've also examined the differences between the self-awareness of men and women and how, whether you search it out or not, the statistics are so stark that the information will find you anyway. Finally, you considered the differences between introverts, who operate on a think-talk-think basis, and extroverts, who operate on a talk-think-talk basis. You've considered the impact this has on the effort required to be reflective and the need for leaders to be inclusive.

Next, you're going to head on to the second leg of your journey – defining and describing leadership.

We have lift-off in 10... 9... 8... 7...

3. WHAT IS LEADERSHIP?

Chapter Map

This leg of the journey takes you through the hills and dales of the land of leadership. You'll explore the history of leadership and the twists and turns the concept has taken over the last 90 years, and what exactly leader effectiveness means in this book. You'll also travel through the valley of hard skills and the peaks of relational skills to better understand their differences and connections and how people's views of them have changed over time. You'll also explore the shadows that leaders cast, considering their impact on others, their organisations and, ultimately, themselves. Before you pull into the pit stop, you'll navigate through the nature-versus-nurture debate to understand whether leaders are born or made and whether leadership is a lesson that can be learnt.

Mirror, signal and let's manoeuvre...

The Journey of Leadership

I can remember hearing the term 'leadership' being bandied about in the early noughties. At the time, I thought it was related to senior management roles, and maybe back then it was. As time has moved on, so has the thinking about leadership and what is meant by the word 'leader'. This isn't the case for all people in all organisations, of course. Some people are firmly fixed in the model of command and control.

But, if you've had an interest in leadership and have been following its development, you'll have perceived the gradual shift.

The discussion about leadership has been going on for almost as long as the discussion about self-awareness. Leadership is one of the most comprehensively researched and debated topics in the organisational sciences.[1] This is because the success of all economic, political and organisational systems depends on the effectiveness of their leaders.[2] The systematic study of leadership began in the early 1930s,[3] and it continues to be an active field of research.[4] I mean, here you are, right?

The specific themes and topics that have been the focus of discussion under the wider leadership umbrella have been changing, though. In the mid-'50s, 'leadership traits' were all the rage. Since then, the trend has moved towards a discussion about leadership styles, which is more focussed on a descriptive or prescriptive way of thinking about leadership.[5]

The Covid-19 pandemic of 2020 changed everything. We were already in an environment where leadership was more about building leader capabilities to manage change and complexity,[6] but 2020 took us *waaay* beyond complexity to crisis. There are five principles for leadership during a crisis: stay calm, communicate, collaborate, co-ordinate and support.[7] To be able to stay calm, a leader needs to operate from a place of deliberate calm[8] and to do that, a leader needs to understand their response to and behaviour in a crisis. And this can't happen without self-awareness, made up of all three layers of the definition: reflection, recognition and regulation. You can't rely on introspection or outrospection alone to get you through a crisis.

It's likely you'll have come across transactional, transformational and charismatic leadership models. They were the leadership buzzwords in the office 20 years ago. Now, the talk is more about strategic leadership and inclusive leadership alongside servant and authentic leadership. Both authentic and servant leadership models reference the importance of self-awareness. You can't be authentic unless you know what you think, feel and value. You can't serve others unless you have an awareness of how you need to behave in service to them.

The model most relevant to self-aware leadership is resonant leadership because it's based on emotional intelligence. It was developed by Daniel Goleman, Richard Boyatzis and Annie McKee and first appeared in their book *Primal Leadership* in 2001. As you know, self-awareness and emotional intelligence are often used interchangeably. If emotional intelligence accounts for 85 to 90% of the difference between average and outstanding leaders (according to Goleman), this model of leadership helps us describe what effective self-aware leadership is. And once you know what it is, you can help people develop their skills to operate in a resonant way.

"People won't go along with you unless they can get along with you."
John C. Maxwell

Resonant leadership is reliant on positive relationships,[9] and as you know from the three-layer definition of self-awareness, self-awareness underpins effective relationships between people. Resonant leaders are described as those that are 'in sync' with those around them and in tune with other people's thoughts and emotions.[10] Resonant leaders are "empathetic, passionate, committed and have the ability to read people and groups accurately".[11] They appreciate the impact of positive interpersonal relationships and understand the emotions of people around them and empower them.[12] Being that we know "emotions are contagious",[13] other people's emotions and behaviours impact people's work performance, which means if you want to relate, resonate!

In my research, I was clear that I was exploring leader effectiveness, not effective leaders, not leadership in general nor anything else connected with leading. I was interested in the leader as an individual. I wanted to understand the impact and influence of the individual first and foremost, then an individual in relation to another person, then a team and then an organisation. If you like, my frame of reference begins with I and ends with us. 'I, we, us': that's my concept of human interaction; it radiates out from I.

"People won't go along with you unless they can get along with you."

John C. Maxwell

My definition of leadership is:

The ability to influence and motivate people and move them towards a common goal by enabling others to contribute to the effectiveness and success of an organisation.[14]

When I'm talking about leadership, this is what I mean. From what I've learnt over the last few years about leadership, the word 'organisation' could easily be swapped for community, team or family.

One of the top takeaways from my discussion with Liam Maguire (episode 19) is that if an organisation is doing well, it's probably down to leadership. If an organisation isn't doing very well, it's probably down to… well, leadership!

Hard Skills vs Relational Skills

One of my favourite ideas is… 'It's not what you do, it's the way that you do it,' which I mentioned earlier in the book. Simply, leadership is what you do and self-awareness is how you do it.

A paper by Mackenzie (1988)[15] describes two types of knowledge that fit well with this idea of what and how. They describe first-order knowledge and second-order knowledge or, to you and me, hard skills and soft skills. First-order knowledge is described as knowledge of an object, process or craft, which can be transmissible and teachable, like a technical skill – think of fixing a bicycle puncture. Second-order knowledge is made up of the emotions and behaviours described as non-technical skills, e.g. beliefs, professionalism, attitudes, personality traits, socio-emotional factors, wisdom, motivation and teamwork.[16] Second-order emotions and behaviours are not transmissible in the same way as first-order technical knowledge and capabilities – think of making the decision to stop and help someone whose bicycle has a puncture.

You'll have noticed that in this chapter, 'hard skills' and 'relational skills' are the terms used. Well, that's because the term 'soft skills' isn't very helpful and a real contradiction in terms! Soft skills are the most difficult to acquire, and by calling them 'soft', it doesn't convey just how difficult they are to develop and maintain. It also perpetuates this false machismo, anti-fluffy stuff mentality where men don't share their emotions, which we know is detrimental to good mental health.

I did a highly unscientific LinkedIn poll in 2021 asking for ideas for a better term than soft skills, and this is how people voted:

- **Relational skills - 35%**
- **Resonant skills - 16%**
- **Emotio-social skills - 32%**
- **Something else (add a comment) - 16%**

Strangely, I discovered two other live polls asking this same question at the same time, and a number of different posts. That could have been thanks to the LinkedIn algorithm, or it might have just been a sign of the times. These are some of the suggestions I found across LinkedIn and ideas for alternative terms people posted in comments to my poll:

- **Behavioural attributes**
- **Core qualities**
- **Crucial characteristics (Jordan Gross's poll)**
- **Emotional quotient (EQ) indicators**
- **Essential qualities (This was the top of Jordan Gross's poll.)**
- **Foundational skills**
- **Human skills (Simon Sinek's post)**
- **Human technical skills**
- **Intangibles**
- **Interaction intelligence**
- **Inter and intrapersonal skills**
- **Non-negotiables (Jordan Gross's poll)**
- **People practices**
- **People skills**

- **Power skills**

- **Real skills**

- **Response versatility**

I decided to stick with 'relational skills' because 'relational' is more commonly used and understood. So, throughout this book, they'll be referred to as relational skills, unless a study specifically calls them something else.

In *Leadership is Language*, L. David Marquet calls thinking/decision-making work 'bluework' because blue is the colour of calm and creativity. Bluework is done by blueworkers. He calls doing 'execution work' and manual labour 'redwork' because red is the colour of energy and determination. Redwork is done by redworkers. There are significant commonalities between first-order knowledge, hard skills and redwork, and between second-order knowledge, relational skills and bluework.

Some studies say people skills are far more relevant than technical skills.[17] Goleman himself said that when he compared high performers in senior leadership positions, in 90% of their profiles, there was a bias towards emotional intelligence over cognitive skills.[18] Goleman (2004) said emotional intelligence proved to be twice as important as technical skills and intellectual quotient (IQ) for jobs at all levels.

Other studies go one step further and propose that IQ and technical skills are far less important to leadership's success than self-awareness.[19] A line from a study by Klare et al. (2014) describes the confusion that results when people in senior roles have got the technical skills down pat but are lacking the emotional intelligence to read the room: "In really smart places, workplace interactions can be very stupid."[20]

It was interesting listening to what Tracy Myhill (episode 18) said about leadership behaviours and how things have changed. Tracy's been a CEO in more than one large NHS organisation so has 'been there, done that and got the T-shirt'. She's also sat at the table and seen others wearing similar T-shirts. She said that people rise to strategic-level roles in all sorts of ways, maybe because of their expertise, or qualifications, or their acute understanding of the business. But, she said, in latter years it's become clear – it's not just what you know that's important in leadership, but how you show up and how you lead. She suggested you are less likely to get into leadership positions these days if you don't focus on values, behaviours and awareness as well as technical knowledge and expertise. She said that compassionate leadership is at the forefront more than ever before. And Tracy lived through healthcare leadership during Covid, so she really has seen it first hand.

The approach in this book is that you have to have hard skills and relational skills. Just like L. David Marquet says, to be effective, we need to weave back and forth between thinking-bluework and doing-redwork. But, in this book, relational skills take precedence. The percentage weighting changes depending on the sector, industry, team, job function and job level you're at, and probably the problem you're trying to solve at any given time, but relational skills need to be considered a minimum of 51% of the time or more. For all you lawyers out there, it's an 'on the balance of probabilities' thing, not a 'beyond reasonable doubt' thing.

The Shadow of a Leader

One of the reasons why it's important to cultivate self-awareness is 'impact', both on others (the behaviour you're putting out) and on yourself (the behaviour that comes back in consequence). When you think about the impact of senior leaders, their impact radiates much further than just the people within their immediate vicinity. Their role elevates them to such a position that their impact, power, influence and shadow extend well beyond the reach of their outstretched arms. Sally Evans (episode 2), an experienced business psychologist and organisation development and strategic HR professional, used the phrase "When you're in leadership, you cast a long shadow." It's absolutely true. So where does this power come from?

Julie Diamond, president of Diamond Leadership, identifies four sources of power, which come from the 1960s model by French and Raven[21]:

- **Positional power from the job description.** Positional power comes from the terms and conditions of the employment contract and the roles and responsibilities set out in the job description.

- **Expert power from knowledge and expertise.** Expert power comes from hard technical skills and expertise from first-order knowledge, and it occasionally puts people in the accidental leadership role. More on that later.

- **Referent power from relationships with others.** Referent power often relies on who you play golf with, who's who in your family and social circle and generally hobnobbing with the great and the good.

- **Personal power from personality and emotional intelligence.** Personal power comes from your ability to influence. Some leaders use loaded guns to influence, some use big fat bonus cheques and others rely on praise, acknowledgement, gratitude and maybe a promotion, if you're lucky.

But power ultimately comes from followers: the people who have to or want to accept your power and be influenced by it.

Relationships between leaders and followers are key to leader effectiveness.[22] Matthew Phelan (episode 13) said that, at the end of the day, if a leader pays someone's wage, like it or not, they have power over them. Alison Lagier (episode 7), a retired NHS leader, said that when you're in a senior position, just walking into a room has an impact.

Having position power through your job title doesn't mean you're actually able to influence people, though. My French teacher in secondary school comes to mind. Throwing board rubbers at non-compliant teenagers was about using position power to compensate for a lack of personal power. I'm sure you'll have come across teachers whose job descriptions gave them the power to lead a class but their inability to influence meant the class just ate them alive. There are plenty of people with the job title who lack the relational skills to actually influence, so when they walk into a room, people don't even notice.

From the feedback I received during my research, it was evident people thought leaders had a lack of awareness of the impact of their position power and underestimated the impact of their decisions. You've probably been in situations where colleagues have tried to influence change in their organisation and in the end said "Sod it" and gone somewhere else where they were more likely to be valued, heard and appreciated. You might have been in this situation yourself.

It's up to each individual leader to activate their power through their behaviour. Alison said leaders should always ask, "What will be the impact on the staff?" She said that leaders need to be adaptable, they need to listen and they need to have a genuine desire to understand other people's points of view. They need to find a way to talk to colleagues about their goals and be aware of the impact their behaviour has on other people. If they don't have awareness of their behaviours, they're not going to be able to bring people along the journey with them and they're not going to be able to achieve their goals. More on this when we talk about inclusive decision making later.

The Nature vs Nurture Debate

Are leaders born or made? The nature–nurture debate is alive and well in the leadership field. A number of studies promote the view that leadership can be learnt,[23] and others say it is an innate ability: "It is who people are – not what they know or how bright they are" that leads to success.[24] People who responded to my research questionnaire and people I interviewed said they felt training couldn't make an individual into a leader. They said training courses couldn't change personalities and behaviours. One interviewee said, "I'm not convinced that any amount of training will make you into a leader if you've not got that in you to start with."[25]

There has to be a hint of a speck of a glimmer of something in an individual which, whether they know it's there or not, can be nurtured and cultivated through training. Jacqui Frost (episode 9) said that to take on leadership functions, you need to elevate your perspective and thinking, and not everybody wants to be in that position. That's why it's so important to give people greater exposure to leadership opportunities in the world of work rather than just providing them with training. Training is often textbook, classroom-type learning, and if learning in this way doesn't float your boat, whether you have hidden innate abilities or not, training isn't going to unlock it for you. Where you've got organisations that operate in a more 'complex adaptive system' way, experiential learning through exposure to on-the-job leadership learning is much more achievable. More on that shortly.

Talent management strategies need to make sure organisations are giving people the chance to unlock their innate abilities across all neurodiversity and skills. If the only leadership training in your organisation is classroom learning and writing assignments, how then will the people who can enthuse a team, plan and strategise well but cannot read and write well even have an opportunity to get a foot in the door?

A number of podcast guests have talked about 'little leaders': children who are demonstrating leadership capabilities. Both Jacqui Frost (episode 9) and Sophie Bryan (episode 17) talked about the leadership behaviours you see in young children. Some children can be observed gathering groups together, showing empathy, advocating for quieter voices, facilitating collaboration, achieving consensus and helping friends expand on ideas. This definitely supports the view that leadership is an innate ability that can be honed and developed through training, not created by going to the right training courses. I mean, at that age, we may have taught children about kindness, turn-taking and sharing but we won't have told them about team dynamics or humility in team captainship. They will have observed it somewhere, absorbed it somehow and have the innate abilities to emulate it. It's leadership by osmosis, and when leadership skills are taken on board at this age, they will be building and strengthening their neural pathways for later life.

You need to nurture the nature that is present in people. The trick is to spot the natural talent and innate abilities! Create greater opportunities for people to let their talents and abilities shine, even if it's just for a moment!

In the Rear-View Mirror

Let's take a pit stop and pause to review the journey you've been on. Readjust the rear-view mirror to make sure you have an unobstructed view.

You've taken a trip into the history of leadership to understand how you got from way back there to right up here. You've read about the trend change from traits to styles. You've explored resonant leadership with its foundations in emotional intelligence and discussed its importance to self-aware leadership. You've explored the definition of leader effectiveness and understood that the perspective of this book starts with I and ends with us.

You've journeyed through the land of leadership, up the hill of hard skills and down the dale of soft skills. You've learnt about how the term 'relational skills' emerged and how it fits better here in this book, being that soft skills are the hardest to acquire. Calling them 'soft' is a misnomer that perpetuates an unhelpful stance.

You've explored the shadows cast by leaders and the increasing impact they have the higher up the organisation they are. You've considered the functional responsibilities and authorities vested through a job description and the realities of leadership without influence. You've joined in the discussion about followership and how titled leaders without willing followers are not leaders at all.

You finished by jumping into the nature-versus-nurture debate and the argument of whether leaders are born or made. You have a clear view that, in this book, leadership is viewed as an innate ability that might require some unearthing and nurturing to be fully revealed. Your last exploration before turning back to the road ahead was a discussion about little leaders and how many children demonstrate leadership capabilities without formal leadership training, suggesting that nature rules and nurture provides the tools.

The bullet train leaves the platform in four seconds...

4. WHERE ARE THE LEADERS?

Chapter Map

Where are the leaders? Before we can answer that, we need to describe the organisations, environments and locations in which they might be. We'll do that by setting out the Five Functions Job Level Framework, which aims to help stratify organisations of different shapes and sizes, with no commonality of structure or job titles. Then we can start to answer the question.

First you'll explore leaders in senior roles: those with leadership titles, responsibilities and accountabilities vested in them by virtue of their job descriptions and employment contracts. Then you'll explore leadership as a function of those without formal leadership positions but who exude an influence that means people want to follow them regardless. Next you'll investigate leadership at all levels and explore complexity leadership operating in complex adaptive systems as an increasingly popular way of creating the right conditions for different leaders to lead at different times and for different purposes.

Let's take a left out onto the superhighway and journey to a place you might never have been before.

The Five Levels of an Organisation

One of the experiences I had that set me on the road to exploring self-aware leadership was with the Road Blocks, introduced to you in Chapter 1, who spanned four levels of organisational hierarchy. Because of that, through my research I wanted to get a picture of self-awareness and leader effectiveness across the whole span of the organisational hierarchies, from the frontline operational staff to the strategic-level executives. You'll have heard me mention strategic-level leaders earlier in this book, so let me explain exactly what I mean, why I give them that name and where it all comes from.

Every organisation in the Welsh public sector is structured differently, and I suspect that will be the same in all organisations across the globe. To be able to stratify my questionnaire findings into a common structure, I first had to develop one. Following lots of research into organisational stratification, hierarchies and testing the model as part of my pilot questionnaire, the final model I settled on was the Five Functions Job Level Framework (FFJLF). It's not the catchiest of titles, but when you're presenting academic work, it has to do what it says on the tin. Maybe that's a challenge I can put to you – can you come up with a sexier name for it? My email address is at the back of the book!

The FFJLF is made up of the following five levels:

Strategic – The most senior level of responsibility within an organisation: setting its strategic direction, making ultimate policy decisions and implementing significant organisational change (e.g. directors, deputy directors, executives, vice presidents, chiefs).

Senior Management – Have overall responsibility for the implementation of organisational policies, procedures and budgets across a number of service areas and influencing the strategic direction of the organisation (e.g. heads of departments, senior managers)

Management – Make sure organisational policies and procedures are implemented; they will have overarching financial responsibility for services (e.g. second- and third-line managers).

Business – Responsible for managing the business of the organisation – for example, signing off timesheets, developing staff rotas, approving leave and conducting sickness interviews. May have some direct contact with service users and clients (e.g. team leaders, supervisors, first-line managers).

Operational – Have direct contact with service users and clients. Have no line management responsibility (e.g. recycling operatives, first-line nurses, social workers, teachers, speech and language therapists, doctors, police constables). Take note though, the salary of operational staff is not always an indicator of their position within the levels, as many operational staff, such as doctors and teachers, will be viewed as 'well paid' even though they have direct contact with service users. Staff within this job level will have no supervisory responsibilities and won't line manage anyone.

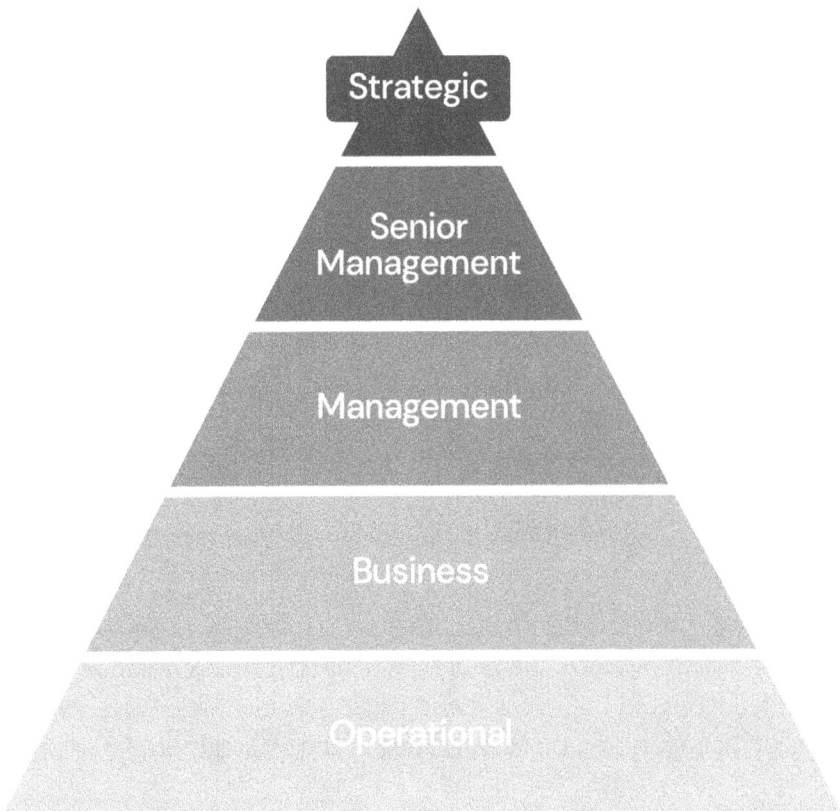

This framework won't overlay perfectly onto all organisations. The smaller the organisation, the more likely it is that roles will straddle more than one level. When there are three of you in a company, the CEO takes on the role of head cook and bottle washer at any given moment and straddles four, if not five, of the layers. Your job in your organisation may straddle two layers or, if you're in a global organisation with thousands of employees, you may find there are levels within levels. But it gives a basic framework to work with into which many or most organisational roles can fit most of the time. Can you identify where you fit? Are you bang in the centre of a level, or do you straddle more than one? Are there a few levels within the levels in your organisation?

When I refer to strategic-level leaders throughout the book, this is where I place these roles in relation to the other four levels.

The Seniority vs Leadership Debate

The traditional view of leadership in the 'industrial paradigm', stretching from the late 18th century to the early 21st century, is that it's synonymous with the functions of those at the strategic level of the organisation. Leadership research has generally focussed on people within roles at this level. The self/other ratings studies that you read about earlier were predominantly interested in these very people, or those in training to take on strategic-level roles.

Out of interest, I wanted to know what the contemporary paradigm was called, so I asked the internet and I got back 'the post-industrial paradigm' or 'the knowledge-based paradigm'. The former is a bit dowdy, and the latter seems a bit more hip, so I'm going to be sticking with that from here on in! It's the time period from the late 20th century, overlapping the industrial paradigm, and it continues to flow into the 21st century.

In general, the literature conceptualises leadership as seniority, and in today's world of work, that still rings true. If you ask most people to name the leaders in their teams and organisations, they'll give you the names of managers and those operating at the strategic level.

The literature links seniority with high levels of EQ.[1] Directors have been found to have significantly higher emotional intelligence scores than managers.[2] High-performing managers have been found to be more able to accurately assess their own behaviours in the workplace.[3] Studies have said things like:

"Emotional intelligence tends to be hierarchically related."[4]

"… scholars have noted that social skills are essential for executive level leaders; as individuals ascend the organizational hierarchy, social intelligence becomes an increasingly relevant determinant of who will and will not be successful."[5]

"The higher one rises in an organization the more self-awareness lies at the centre of leadership development."[6]

"EI levels are higher among workplace leaders, and are even further elevated as leadership levels rise in an organization."[7]

A correlation between salary, job level and emotional intelligence has been explored, and a correlation has been found.[8] The researchers based their thinking on the idea that emotionally intelligent individuals are more able to develop strong interpersonal relationships, networking skills, and political acumen, which lead to career progression.

Why am I telling you all this? I want to describe to you just how heavy the weight of academic opinion is on this point of whether leaders at the most strategic level of organisations have greater self-awareness than leaders at other levels of organisations. This is because what I discovered in my research, and what people were telling me and are continuing to tell me, is the opposite.

My questionnaire data suggested that leaders at the strategic job level had less self-awareness than effective leaders identified at any of the other four job levels. One research interviewee said, "There are very intelligent people who have no ability to understand their own behaviour and impact on other people."

In year one of my podcast, I asked every guest the question, "Do you think leaders at the most strategic level of organisations have greater self-awareness than leaders at other levels of organisations?" Most started their answers with a wry chuckle and went on to say, "I don't think so", "No", or "I wish the answer was yes."

Leaders with Titles vs Leaders Without

"Leadership is not about an individual in a senior role, it is about many people across an organisation involved in leadership activities." [9]

Even though leadership as seniority is the most common stance taken in the literature, it isn't the only one. Some scholars are challenging the idea that leadership and seniority are synonymous and that leadership rests solely with people in supervisory roles.[10] I'm really glad this is the case, and it certainly reflects my experience of the Fairy Goth Mother and people like her.

Síle Walsh (episode 14) said that titled leadership comes with position power, and it's created by organisational structures. It generally puts titled leaders at the top of people-teams and organisational functions. Social leadership, however, creates leaders everywhere. Social leaders are created through followership. Síle said that, ideally, what we want is social leaders in titled leadership positions.

Alison Lagier (episode 7) also talked about social leaders, referring to them as 'unofficial influencers', saying they can both help and derail the achievement of goals in an organisation. If an unofficial influencer has followers, those followers will follow that individual towards the will of the organisation or against it. Unofficial influencers can be skilled at listening, speaking confidently, detangling others' challenges and presenting those challenges to others. They're often able to articulate issues on behalf of others. They are intuitively skilled at bringing people together. These are traits I saw in the Fairy Goth Mother.

Tracy Myhill (episode 18) listed similar traits and behaviours: they trust those around them, are open, engaging, look out for people, spot stressed people who are struggling, help, suggest development opportunities for others (even their seniors), are honest, give honest feedback, can connect, understand their people, care for their team members and they're collaborative not competitive. Alison said it's important for senior-level managers and executives to recognise these individuals and bring them along on the journey to achieving goals. It's important to find the people with the skills and give them the opportunity to lead and represent others.

Leadership at All Levels

Discussions about complex adaptive systems and complexity leadership are creating a groundswell of movement away from the traditional industrial paradigm model. A complex adaptive system is a system of organisations, teams, companies or 'parts' that interact and are interdependent. If you do an online search for an example of a complex adaptive system, you'll get suggestions like an ant colony, a social network and an economy. These are systems that adapt in response to both internal and external influences such as where food sources are, the main topics of news and current affairs, local disasters, population changes and global financial downturns. The UK National Health Service system is structured so that a patient has to go to their general practitioner first, then is referred for tests, and the results of the tests dictate whether they need to see a consultant or not. This is a more structured system and has less stimulus for adaptation. That is until you throw a global crisis like a pandemic into the mix, of course, and then it quickly adapts for the benefit of the furtherance of the human race.

> **"Complex adaptive systems are defined as neural-like networks of interacting, interdependent agents who are bonded together in a collective dynamic by a common need."** [11]

Complexity leadership theory is the idea that leadership has to respond to internal and external influences and interdependencies. It's essentially the kind of leadership that operates in a complex adaptive system and has to respond to the challenges of these internal and external influences and interdependencies whilst making sure the organisation continues to run effectively. It supports the idea that leadership is and should be at all levels and moves the thinking away from individuals in senior roles to whole systems[12] that need to change direction to be responsive. In changing direction, the system might need different people leading at different times.

Research in the late 2010s was more interested in relational, dynamic and distributed leadership processes, which is a step away from the more traditional view of leadership being linked to the traits, characteristics and behaviours of a senior individual.[13] When researchers and academics talk about relational types of leadership, they refer to models like collaborative, distributed, shared and complexity theories.[14] The whole discussion is far more focussed on relationships than individuals. Individuals are considered to be evolving alongside each other as part of a wider system, and it's the system as a whole that's the focus of attention rather than the individuals who make up that system.[15] The discussion is more interested in where people's journeys intersect, cross over, split off and join again rather than the individuals on those journeys, per se.

It's the spaces between people that are key to leadership, i.e. it's the relationships and connections between people, rather than the actions of people themselves, that are important.[16] This reference to 'spaces between' takes you back to the three-layer definition of self-awareness – reflection, recognition and regulation. If you think of a Venn diagram, the overlap would be the spaces between individuals where recognition would also live.

Relations-orientated leadership involves showing concern for the welfare of people in job levels below yours, recognising and appreciating their work contribution and also involving them in making decisions.[17] But positive relationships should not be seen as devoid of conflict[18] and will become relevant later when we explore care, authenticity and feedback. "… complexity theory suggests that appropriate amounts of heterogeneity in terms of thought diversity and exposure to ideological differences is conducive to adaptive behavior."[19] This is something that Matthew Syed also talks about in his book *Rebel Ideas*. You need cognitive diversity to help you get away from groupthink and find the best solutions to problems. This resonates with what Brené Brown says about "rumbling with vulnerability". She talks about needing to get down in the dirt and thrash out problems and disagreements together in respectful and safe places to help you work shit out!

This takes us on to the concept of 'systems thinking'. There has been a shift from the idea of an 'organisation as a biological model to a sociocultural model' and a shift from analytical thinking to systems thinking.[20] If we're moving from an industrial paradigm where organisations did their own thing, information flowed up and down and decisions were made at the top, we need to explore and find out how organisations in the knowledge-based paradigm are operating now and how they will need to do things differently in the future.

Systems thinking is considered a cognitive intelligence.[21] Why is that relevant to you? Well, cognitive intelligence is a human's ability to learn, problem solve, and their mental reasoning ability, and it's measured by an IQ assessment. For you, that means systems thinking falls under the first-order knowledge descriptor of 'hard skills'. Systems thinking is a hard skill, and a hard skill can be learnt. It also means it's on the 49% side of your scales, and relational skills still need to be considered for the other 51%.

This idea of leadership at all levels and leadership moving to meet internal and external influences and interdependencies is played out in the Agile management theories like Scrum. They seem to be the PRINCE2 of their day. Agile is based on the idea that priorities and leadership are determined by the success of the previous work phase. This seems like the opposite of PRINCE2, which sets structure and plans in place from here to doomsday.

Now, I've got nothing against PRINCE2. As a born organiser, the whole idea behind it puts me in my comfort zone. But, having lived through Covid and the realities of no one having a clue what comes next, planning on the basis of 'we'll work out what to do tomorrow when we work out the impact of what we did yesterday' seems quite logical. I've had three podcast guests talking about Scrum: Donald Henderson (Scrum master in the NHS), Agile leadership expert Sathpal Singh (together on episode 3) and Gunther Verheyen (episode 5) (author and a leading voice on the Scrum methodology). PRINCE2 and Agile are 'of their time', being developed in 1989 and 2001, respectively. There are good practices to take away from both. There's a 'PRINCE2 Agile' course in existence now, which I assume does exactly that!

Gunther is a master practitioner in this field and has written many books about Scrum. One of my top takeaways from our discussion was the idea that leadership moves to different individuals with different skill sets based on the work at hand. Working within the framework of Scrum (where work programmed develops in response to outputs), outcomes of leadership – and therefore leads – are constantly changing in response to that need. In this way of working, people sort of 'claim' authority without actually having to have hierarchical authority bestowed on them, giving way to consideration of self-managing teams.

If you're not already an enlightened Agile organisation, can you imagine your organisation moving to this kind of distributed leadership model? I can hear the control freaks screaming from here!

More organisations seem to be working in or moving towards a structured-Scrum way. There's still a hierarchy and the FFJLF is infinitely visible, but individuals within organisations are being given a platform, a voice and an opinion in a way they wouldn't have been 20 years ago. There was a real shift in leadership during Covid. Immunologists and infection control professionals led the charge. People in organisations who had never before done so led discussions with teams of hundreds of people or appeared on TV with prime ministers. Different people found themselves in front of us, leading us on a journey when they had no idea where we might be going. Leadership as a concept changed during that time, and it certainly brought home the fact that people at the strategic level of organisations don't have all the answers.

I valued the openness with which Tracy Myhill (episode 18) spoke to me about this. She said Covid was a traumatic, stressful and difficult time, and there wasn't a leader on the planet who'd been down that road before. The leaders who demonstrated humility, engagement and awareness rose to the fore. As terrible as Covid was, it brought out the best in leadership, and some bright, capable people who'd been hidden in the old structures were elevated and demonstrated some amazing leadership.

New organisations and companies that have been established post-dot.com boom are embracing new ways of working, thinking and operating. They are leaning into complexity leadership, complex adaptive system structures and shaping new decision-making processes. Google and Spotify operate with more flexible and autonomous models of decision making. There's an interesting article by Mark Cruth, modern work expert at Atlassian, titled 'Discover the Spotify Model'. He says, "The Spotify model is a people-driven autonomous approach for scaling agile that emphasizes the importance of culture and network."[22] He describes how Spotify is structured into squads, tribes, chapters, guilds, trios and alliances. He also lists the benefits of the Spotify model, saying there are fewer formal processes and ceremonies and more self-management and autonomy. It's definitely worth a read if you're thinking of diversifying your operational practices and governance structures.

In the Rear-View Mirror

You've journeyed along a section of the superhighway you might never have been on before. It's a part of the highway that's becoming increasingly busy as people get to know its benefits.

You set off from the FFJLF, made up of strategic, senior management, management, business and operational levels as a way of trying to establish some commonality across organisations by offering a universal stratifying method. Then you explored the common stance within the literature of leadership being synonymous with seniority, and responsibilities and accountabilities being vested in individuals via job descriptions. You explored studies that evidence increased levels of emotional intelligence and self-awareness in strategic-level roles. You considered the differences between titled leaders and social leaders and the impact of influence in generating followership. You learnt about the importance of social and unofficial leaders in achieving organisational goals.

You then hiked up the hill to explore the concept of complex adaptive systems burgeoning in the knowledge-based paradigm as the functional opposite to traditional 'pyramid-shaped' organisations with affinity to the industrial paradigm. You joined the discussion about complexity leadership as the leadership model present within complex adaptive systems and the changing nature of roles in response to delivery need. You walked around the summit and considered relations-orientated leadership and the importance of the 'spaces between' individuals rather than the skills of the individuals themselves. You read about the need for cognitive diversity as a means of generating effective problem-solving relationships. You heard about systems thinking as a cognitive skill necessary for the effective function of complex adaptive systems, being that they are without formal structures but rather have fluid and changing structures. You leant on your walking poles as you peered into agile operating structures and focussed particularly on Scrum as a helpful methodology for coping with crises and unchartered territory.

Now, jump on my luggage cart as we head to the transfer lounge of Part 1 to sum up your journey so far.

THE TRANSFER LOUNGE: PART 1

"Self-awareness is the magic ingredient to leader effectiveness."
Amy Gandon (episode 15)

You are now at the transfer lounge between Part 1 – 'Why?' and Part 2 – 'Where?', and it's a good opportunity to reflect on the big top takeaways from your journey so far. You've explored self-awareness, leader effectiveness and leadership at all levels, and we now bring them all together to create the model of self-aware leadership, which is central to your journey on the Self-Awareness Superhighway.

The following diagram sets out the three-layer definition of self-awareness alongside the definition of leader effectiveness. It combines internal self-awareness, internal-social self-awareness and external-social self-awareness with hard skills and relational skills to form one easy-to-remember, carry-in-your-pocket, fit-on-a-Post-it-note definition that you can share with others.

"Self-awareness is the magic ingredient to leader effectiveness."

Amy Gandon

DEFINITION OF SELF-AWARENESS	SELF-AWARE LEADERSHIP	DEFINITION OF LEADER EFFECTIVENESS
Internal self-awareness is an ability to recognise the self's changing thoughts, feelings, beliefs, values, strengths and abilities through reflection and introspection.	Reflection of skills	An ability to recognise the self's hard skills and relational skills (i.e. changing thoughts, feelings, beliefs, values, strengths and abilities) through reflection and introspection.
Internal-social self-awareness is an ability to recognise how the self is received by, perceived by and impacts others.	Recognition of impact	An ability to recognise how the self's hard skills and relational skills are received by, perceived by and impact others.
External-social self-awareness is an ability to read and understand the emotions and intentions of others and respond and act wisely in social exchanges.	Regulation of behaviour	An ability to read and understand the emotions and intentions of others and respond and act wisely in social exchanges by regulating the self's hard skills and relational skills.
Our definition of self-aware leadership is...		
=	'reflection, recognition and regulation of hard skills and relational skills'.	=

So, I ask again, **"Why are you here, traveller?"**

- What is your purpose in developing your self-aware leadership skills?
- Why is it important to you?
- What difference will it make to you?
- What difference will it make to others?

Write your answers down somewhere safe so you can return to them at the end of your journey with me. You can reflect on whether your learning journey has provided you with knowledge and ideas to spur the answers you need to chart your map along your Self-Awareness Superhighway.

PART 2
WHERE ARE YOU GOING?

5. THE SELF-AWARENESS COMPASS

Chapter Map

The first part of our journey together is complete. You know what's important and you know why you're here. The next leg of your journey will mean turning off the road ahead and leaving at the next junction. You'll take the slip road down to the interchange, with nine exits heading in nine different directions. You will need to travel all nine routes on your self-aware leadership journey, but you will need to spend more time travelling in some directions than others. Before you decide which of the directions to travel first, you need to know more about each of the nine routes.

To guide your journey, I'll share a unique nine-pointed self-awareness compass to help you chart your map along your superhighway.

These are the nine CHARTABLE compass points of self-aware leadership and the nine directions you will explore:

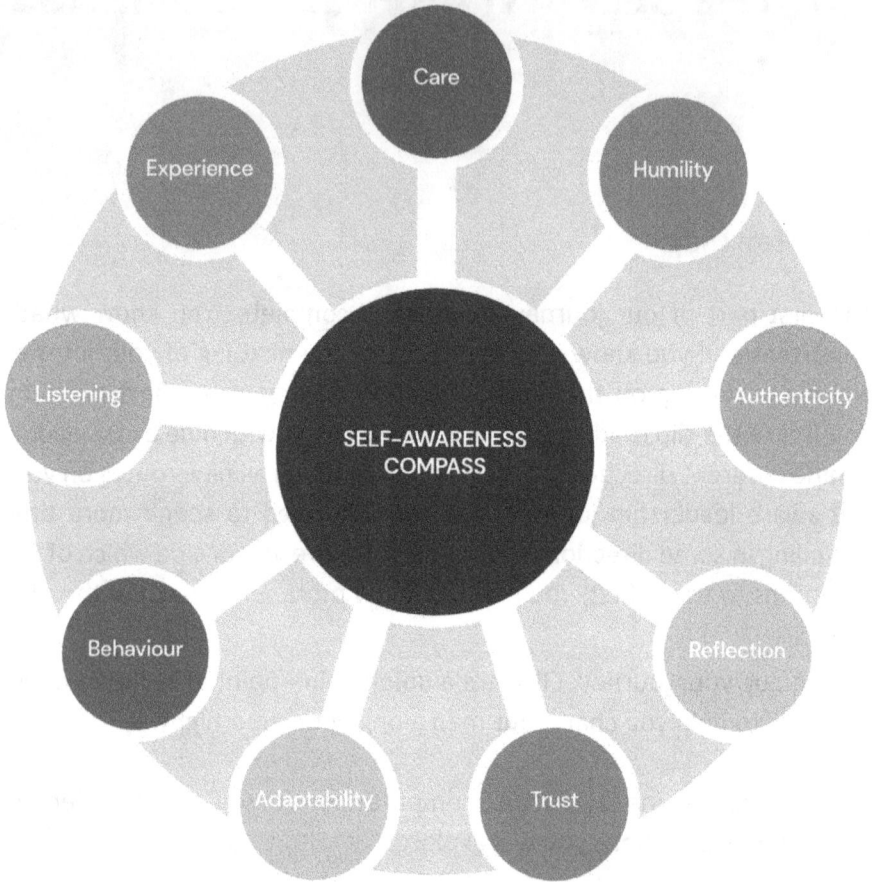

Put your sunglasses on, your water bottle within arm's reach and let's hit the road.

1.   Care

**"Leadership is not about being in charge.
Leadership is about taking care of those in your charge."**
Simon Sinek

Care is one of the most fundamental behaviours all humans need to function well. To maintain your health and happiness, you need to both receive care and show care for others. You don't switch off this need when you step into work, much to the chagrin of the bosses and strategic-level leaders who are gripping hold of the industrial age with their fingernails. Care is as relevant to each of you at work as it is at home, and if you want to be an effective and self-aware leader, you must be able to demonstrate care for others and care for yourself.

As we journey along the superhighway of care, we'll pass the town of kindness, the city of respect and the village of empathy. You can't travel along the route of care without passing these special places, supping the water from their streams and feeling their warm breeze on your face.

Let's journey along route number one and follow the compass point of **care**.

During my research, I interviewed someone who clearly hadn't prepared and, by the surprised sound of their voice, had totally forgotten I was going to be calling them. It was a bit of a meandering, rambling discussion and not everything made sense, but then they said something, and it was as if they'd taken a floodlight and illuminated the midnight sky:

"Ineffective leadership is, you know, it's like a lack of care."

It was said with such genuine and unfettered authenticity that I can still hear their voice in my ear, cutting through the babble with this golden one-liner.

Self-aware leaders care. One of the critical factors when you throw your behaviour out into the world is that you need to care about how it lands with someone else. If you don't care whether your bad behaviour is going to cause upset and worry to someone else, you're certainly not a self-aware leader in my book (pun intended, sorry not sorry).

Don't confuse a caring leader with someone who isn't prepared to have difficult conversations, though. Care is neither sycophantic nor blinkered. If you've listened to the conversation I had with Tom Desch in the anniversary episode of his podcast, *Conversations on Leadership* (9 May 2023), you'll have heard me say that I value leaders who are able to have difficult conversations and not shy away from them. "Embrace the suck" (thanks, Brené Brown) and "feel the fear and do it anyway" (thanks, Susan Jeffers). When leaders care, they're honest with people and don't dodge the discussion about performance or bullying behaviour. They appreciate the sentiment behind being cruel to be kind and care enough to say what needs to be said, respectfully and kindly.

As you already know, my research focussed on the public sector, and it dawned on me that for organisations to provide services to their communities by keeping it healthy, safe, clean, well maintained, sustainable, fed, watered, dry, housed, taught, etc., those organisations had to fundamentally care about their communities. That's what public services are all about, aren't they? Putting in place formalised structures of care, whether that be healthcare, social care, highway maintenance, education... whatever. If you're thinking about organisations that 'do' care in a hard skills kind of way, then surely the organisation itself needs to extend that care in a relational skills kind of way to the employees providing that care? It's a pretty logical step to suggest organisations that care about their customers should also care about their employees. If you have organisations that show no care for their staff, then I'd question whether those organisations are really able to show genuine care for their customers, service users or patients.

Richard Branson said, "If you look after your people, your people will look after your customers." Exactly this. When an organisation's operating premise is having high external standards of care towards customers, they really should mirror these standards of care to the people inside their organisations. This seems especially important in organisations that can't recognise their employees' commitment or high performance through pay rewards and bonuses, like most public-sector organisations. Covid really brought this home, and recognition of health professionals' contribution and commitment became a topic of regular discussion during and since. A national round of applause at 8pm on a Thursday doesn't pay the rent.

A live LinkedIn discussion between Stephen Shedletzky and Tiffani Bova in July 2023 explored the challenges employees face when they aren't valued in organisations and the benefits of balancing customer engagement with internal stakeholder engagement. When your focus of care is weighted towards customers and not balanced between customers and employees, your organisation will suffer the consequences with high staff turnover, low productivity and limited growth.

In the studies exploring complex adaptive systems and relations-orientated leadership, being caring and the impact of being uncaring are very evident. They talk about the importance of demonstrating a concern for subordinates' welfare and wellbeing[1] and how appearing to be uncaring undermines successful leadership.[2] There are leaders in the world who, of course, don't care. My research interviewees talked about people climbing the career ladder and said things like, "People who are nice to your face wouldn't think twice about not supporting you if it didn't benefit them." That probably fits with Tessa West's definition of 'the kiss-up/kick-downer' in her book *Jerks at Work*. But maybe this is the difference between a leader and a self-aware leader. To be a self-aware leader, you must care about your people as individuals, teams and an organisation as a whole. You must constantly be balancing the implementation of policies and procedures to ensure equality and equity for everybody, whilst ensuring that people are valued as individuals.

Some years ago, I was involved in a wholescale restructure of my service. It involved around 100 people and took nearly 18 months to plan, refine and implement. One thing that was very important to me was ensuring I'd had one-to-one conversations with the individuals whose jobs were being disestablished or changed. This was to make sure they knew about things impacting them before anybody else or anything was shared in a group. They needed time to think about the implications for their careers and their families. They needed the opportunity to deal with the emotional impact with as small a number of people in the room as possible so that when the message was shared in a big group of staring eyes, they'd be able to respond in the way they wanted, not react with fight, flight or freeze. Emotionally charged situations should never be a spectator sport. This is one of the ways that self-aware leaders show care: by being respectful and pre-empting the emotional responses of others.

When you consider the layoffs that happened in the global tech industry in 2022–23, you can certainly see the absence of care. There are several reports of people trying to log on to their work network from home one day, only to find they'd been barred access and a follow-up email arriving in their private account an hour or two later saying their job had gone and their contract had been terminated. I don't care what country you're in and what employment law framework exists there – that is a bad way to treat human beings. This shows a reprehensible lack of care, and I'm always shocked and saddened that even if one person thought this was okay, there were 20 others who ratified the approach from across HR and the C-suite. No one pulled the process and said, "We don't behave like that here."

As a self-aware leader, your care of others must be underpinned by respect, both for others and yourself. Behaving respectfully can never be wrong because it sets out who you are and, like it or not, when you're the leader and you're under 24/7 scrutiny, how you behave, how you care and how you show respect for others says more about you than it ever will about them.

Gunther Verheyen (episode 5) said self-awareness was the foundation of empathy, and empathy is necessary to truly understand and develop effective relationships with work colleagues. Without understanding your own drivers and behaviours, you can't have empathy for others and you can't begin to understand their behaviour and your impact on them. If you fail to grasp the essence of empathy, it will impede your ability to develop effective relationships with other people.

Show care; don't hide away from care. Be kind, show empathy and always, always be respectful to others. As a self-aware leader, it's up to you to lead the way in showing what care means in your team and organisation. Model care, expect care and demand care within your organisation.

2.   Humility

**"Humility (noun): Willingness to stay teachable
regardless of how much you already know."**
Shining Wisdom

When you google 'antonym of humility', you get 'arrogance' and 'pride'. Add ego to that list. A self-aware leader is one who doesn't boast and isn't guided by self-aggrandisement and self-interest. Humble leaders encourage other people to shine. They raise others up, nurturing them and encouraging them to play to their strengths, giving them a chance to discover those as yet unearthed skills and abilities. Humility shows a confidence in their own competence, a certainty in their own capability and a vulnerability and openness to learning and improving.

Let's journey along route number two and follow the compass point of **humility**.

Humility is the ability to put your accomplishments and talents into perspective, admitting your fallibility and mistakes and understanding your strong and weak points, seeking contributions from others to overcome your limitations.[3] Or, as John Gottman would say, "Admit when you're wrong. Shut up when you're right." Harsh but true!

Humility was mentioned as being an element of self-awareness in Part 1. There are also other studies that list self-awareness as one of the three dimensions of humility, alongside openness and transcendence.[4] Just like the discussion about self-awareness versus emotional intelligence, there's a similar discussion going on about whether humility is an element of self-awareness or whether self-awareness is an element of humility.

Humility is frequently talked about when describing the servant leadership model. It's described as an internally focussed ability to acknowledge one's limitations[5] that arise from a proper understanding and awareness of one's strengths and weaknesses.[6] That sounds pretty much like internal self-awareness.

Let's consider a leader who we'll call Jo. There are lots of instances where Jo has said, "I'm sorry, that was me," or "I forgot." This demonstrates both humility and vulnerability (which seem to be close bedfellows). You know when people say if you laugh at yourself, no one can laugh at you? Well, Jo has always taken the same approach to admitting their mistakes. They started doing this on the basis that it gave them strength and, occasionally, the upper hand. It was something they consciously did before they knew very much about leadership and even less about humility as a positive leadership behaviour. Jo decided that if they showed humility, they were less likely to have their ego bubble burst. Jo says, "If you've already outed yourself, no one else can out you!" There are plenty of people out there who will be only too willing to point the finger, so Jo's advice is to set out your stall as a humble operator and develop a reputation for admitting your mistakes before anyone else does. The one big caveat Jo would add is to always remember to include that little line about how you're going to fix it too. Be like Jo.

I recall an instance where someone came to me to say they'd put something out on social media and then discovered the language wasn't appropriate and had to take it down. I'm not going to congratulate them for messing up, but I am going to thank them for their candour and for both stopping the problem from escalating and fixing it and being a part of the team that's going to work out what to do to make sure it doesn't happen again. Humility opens the door for this kind of exchange and problem solving. If I'd discovered the cock-up because someone had mentioned it a few weeks later, I'd have been less supportive and would have probably called the individual in for one of those difficult conversations. I appreciate people who come to me and tell me they've messed up. If you've read my blog, you'll know my view that...

"Leadership is about making sure your team know they can mess up with back up."

Would your team say that you create an environment where they feel safe to mess up?

I once worked with a manager who lacked emotional intelligence to a highly frustrating degree. They would support me in one-to-one meetings, but then in large meetings, would say nothing and let the

"Leadership is about making sure your team know they can mess up with back up."

Dr Nia D. Thomas

bus run right over me. I remember once, there were around 20 of us in a large committee room sitting around a huge table in big chairs that made us all look like Lilliputians. I can't remember the discussion, but I can remember how it felt. I can see my manager now. They were sitting opposite me and one to the right. The discussion was going on around the room, and I sat there and waited to see whether they had the initiative or courage to actually say something and show a little bit of allyship. Not a flicker. I was both angry and surprised. Angry that they hadn't backed me and surprised because they knew I knew they'd supported me in private but not in public. Are you having flashbacks of a similar situation? That's the kind of thing that stays with you. When a manager won't help you out of a sticky spot, you're sure as hell not going to help them out when the sticky stuff is being slung at them. What goes around comes around! (See Chapter 1).

In my podcast, a number of guests talk about humility, especially in relation to seeking help from others as a way of sharing knowledge to fix problems and make better decisions. Leadership and management author and teacher Robertson Hunter Stewart (episode 8) said, if you don't know the answer, be confident enough to say so. When you acknowledge what you don't know, you have the chance to learn and develop. When you tell a fib to cover up your lack of knowledge, you'll find yourself in a tricky situation when it's discovered later on, and it will be, for sure!

This absolutely links to the behaviour of integrity too and to Jo's approach to admitting mistakes before someone else points the finger at you. If you've done something that might be causing risk or injury to someone else, realised you've done it and then said nothing about it, you need to take a long hard look at what integrity means for you and where you are on the journey to living it.

Confidence or a lack of it has a significant impact on your ability to lead and lead well. My research interviewees said leader effectiveness was made up of self-awareness and confidence, and a lack of confidence equated to ineffective leadership. A lack of confidence was also seen as a barrier, "preventing sensitive, respectful individuals progressing through the job levels".

Jon Rennie (episode 11) said he feels humility opens the door to learning. If you're humble enough to listen to your critics, you might just stumble on those nuggets to help you learn, develop and improve. As a leader, you need to accept that you don't have the answers to everything, but you do need to listen long enough to know what questions you should be asking. That also connects humility to listening (compass point number seven).

I did a little poll on social media, across LinkedIn, Facebook and Reddit, to see how people felt about humility within their working world:

Humility is the key to effective self-aware leadership.

It allows leaders to acknowledge their strengths and weaknesses, embrace feedback and learn from their experiences.

Is humility valued in your organisation?

- **Absolutely not - 14%**
- **Rarely - 14%**
- **A little - 16%**
- **Every single day - 56%**

I'm not sure how I feel about these results. Saddened that only 56% of people felt humility was living and breathing in their organisations, or glad that 86% of people felt humility was valued to a greater or lesser extent? Where would you put your organisation?

As you develop your self-awareness, you reduce the size of your blind spot and become enlightened about just how much you don't know. When you have this kind of awareness of how little you know in comparison to how much about the world there is to know, you can't but be humble and vulnerable. Being a humble leader is not only good for you, it's good for others too because it gives them the opportunity to problem solve and make decisions together with you. It gives you the opportunity to learn, grow and become better whilst demonstrating that you have confidence in your abilities and the strength to be humble and vulnerable. It's a virtuous cycle and models the kind of open behaviour you want to see in others and your teams.

3.   Authenticity

"Authenticity is the alignment of head, mouth, heart, and feet –
thinking, saying, feeling, and doing the same thing – consistently.
This builds trust, and followers love leaders they can trust."
Lance Secretan, as shared by Sarah Fisher, HR Business Consultant,
on LinkedIn, May 2023

Who are you? What do you think about? What's important to you? What are you good at? What are you not good at? If you don't know the answers to these questions, your self-awareness is not as developed as you might want it to be. If you want to be a self-aware leader who resonates with their colleagues, you need to work out the answers to all these questions and then keep reflecting on those answers. Be cognisant of when your answers change.

Being authentic isn't about wearing your sequined Saturday night clubbing jacket into work on a Monday or doing your Thursday night comedy club routine in the canteen on a Tuesday. Being authentic is about peeling all these things away and working out who you are, who you want to be around others and what reputation you want to create. Which of your thoughts, opinions and views are you happy sharing in the workplace? Which ones will allow you to be the best work-version of yourself, where you can have meaningful relationships with other people and go home at the end of your day knowing you've represented your values and stuck to your principles in a way that benefits you, your colleagues and you?

Let's journey along route number three and follow the compass point of **authenticity** to help work out who the authentic work-you really is.

The word authenticity is bandied about with wild abandon, which is a little disappointing. There's a 'Short' on YouTube by Red Team Thinking in which they share a clip of someone saying, "When a word develops a capital letter, you know it's dead." In contemporary business speak, it's no longer authenticity, it's 'Authenticity!'. Maybe because the idea of being authentic was so frowned upon in days gone by, we're pushing the pendulum in the totally opposite direction in the hope that when it swings and comes to rest, it'll be somewhere in the middle. 'Leave your troubles at the door' is now 'Bring your whole self to work.' Well, sometimes it just doesn't feel right to wear your sequined Saturday night jacket to your co-working space.

It's also thought that because the business world has gone through some really high-profile 'ethical meltdowns'[7] and legal crises in the last 20 years, authenticity has been pushed to the top of the effective leadership behaviours list by necessity.

> **"Authentic leadership is a relevant concept that satisfies a current public need for accountability, integrity, courage and transparency because of its focus on leaders' own transparency, internal principles and a moral compass in the face of nefarious, shifting and possibly ethically ambiguous business practices."** [8]

Authenticity is about expressing your true self.[9] You need to understand your 'multi-faceted self-nature' and own your "thoughts, emotions, needs, wants, preferences and beliefs".[10] Or, you might say, to be an authentic leader, you need to be internally self-aware. At the heart of authentic leadership is "self-awareness, openness, transparency, and consistency".[11] You need to be anchored by your own deep sense of self.[12] Authentic leadership is underpinned by the belief "To thine own self be true" (Shakespeare, 1901: *Hamlet*, Act I Scene iii).[13] Authentic leaders tell the truth and are trusted; they do what they say they're going to do,[14] which links trust to integrity. They're also high in moral character.[15]

The idea of 'relational transparency' is also an element of authentic leadership, and if it begins with 'relational', it must be relevant to self-aware leadership! It's described as the leader's ability to present an authentic self, rather than a fake or distorted self, to promote trust.[16] This idea of being 'in relation' aligns well with what we're talking about in this book. I've already said you can't be self-aware unless you're interacting with others and being given that opportunity to see yourself through the eyes of another. Reflecting on your behaviour as a solo activity is introspection. Reflecting on your behaviour with the insight of someone else gives you recognition and regulation: you can't have all three layers when it's just you. It's the same for leadership – you can't be a leader in an empty room.

To be authentic, a leader needs to understand themselves in relation to others and they need ongoing feedback and clarification from others.[17] Leader authenticity has a significant impact on employees and, in turn, the authenticity of both leader and employees contribute to the health and climate of an organisation.[18] To borrow a phrase from the erudite Julian Stodd, "It's an ecosystem."

In your network, there will be people who hold confidences like a bank vault, and there will be those who can't keep a secret to save their lives. There will be people who will drop a familiar word into a discussion and you'll just know that the word has come from you! You have to be a different you when you're around them. "How do you square this with being authentic?" you ask. Well, we are all a myriad of things, and you can draw on your authentic self to be all these different 'yous' without betraying your beliefs, values and priorities.

I had a Welsh teacher who was very old school. They wore an academic's black cape most of the time, used chalk on the board and taught us grammar by making us write sentences from poems over and over again. Everything we knew about them was from stories by others. Their father had been the school headmaster many years before, a strict authoritarian, so I hear. They'd been engaged to marry but their father had prevented it. Shortly after, their fiancé drowned themself by walking into the sea with rocks in their pockets. My teacher was a faith healer and connected in some way to the Church. The stories were both fascinating and tragic. As children, did we even know what their favourite colour or food was or where they went on holiday? No. No idea. Their relationship with us would have been so much warmer and kinder had they just admitted that KitKats were their favourite chocolate and they kept a box in their cupboard for break times. I watched how the other teachers interacted with them, and even at 14 or 15, I could see there was a detachment from them too. They lived behind a mask and authenticity was a galaxy away. Occasionally, the staffroom door would open and I would see the awkward shuffle others made so as not to bump into them whilst they had a cup of tea in hand and a KitKat balanced on the saucer.

You can define authenticity as the extent to which an individual is true to their core values and acts in accordance with those values.[19] If you don't know what your core values are, you can't act in accordance with them. If you tell people what your values are and then don't have the self-awareness to be able to behave in a way that lives those values, what you say will be hollow and meaningless, and people will hear the inauthenticity in your voice like an alarm bell. To be authentic, you've actually got to mean what you say.

Alison Smith (episode 4) is a speaker and trainer who expertly uses metaphor to help people get unstuck. She said the more self-aware you become, the more layers you're able to peel away to reveal your authentic self. When people appreciate that your behaviour is coming from a place of awareness and authenticity, they are more able to respond positively to you. People can smell a fake a mile off. Being disingenuous does not endear you to anybody. Alison said that when people cover themselves in layers and mask their true selves, it makes relationship forming much more difficult. She said you have to own and accept all of your parts, good and bad.

Peeling back layers is a curious activity in leadership, though. You have to be sure you're taking off as many layers as you can cope with. You need to find that balance between sharing and retaining. As a leader, you're going to have to handle some difficult things, like performance management, disciplinaries, restructures and redundancies. When you know these things are on the horizon, the last thing you need is to become so emotionally connected to your colleagues that it clouds your judgement and means you can't do your job as well as you would want. I spent nearly eight years in my longest job, and I saw people go through weddings, pregnancies, funerals, divorces, arguments and promotions. I definitely became incredibly fond of and cared greatly for my team. But for my own self-care and to make sure I could deal with the emotionally difficult situations I knew would come sooner or later, I stepped back from going to some of the team's social events – like celebratory meals out, hen dos, 30th birthday trips to Magaluf – as I moved up the career ladder. I guess you could say I had to put some of the onion layers I'd peeled off back on. You need to be able to balance authenticity with self-preservation, and I'm not hearing too many people talking about that.

You need to be authentic to be a self-aware leader and to be self-aware means you are able to be authentic. Not in a supercilious 'no jacket is too sequined, no joke is too risqué' kind of way, but in a 'these are the things that are important to me, these are my values, this is what I want my reputation to be' kind of way. The really important things.

4.   Reflection

"By three methods, we may learn wisdom:
First, by reflection, which is noblest;
Second, by imitation, which is easiest;
and third, by experience, which is the bitterest."
Confucius

One of the critical elements that makes self-aware leadership different to other leadership models is reflection. Other models do, of course, reference reflection, but when self-awareness is by definition made up of reflection, recognition and regulation, then reflection as a concept and an activity sits at the heart of self-aware leadership. This book is predicated on the worldview that both self-awareness and leadership are socially constructed concepts, which means they both can only happen fully when there are relationships between people: when there is you and others. You can't be self-aware without insight and feedback from someone else, and you can't be a leader when others don't choose to follow you. The self-aware leadership model needs relationships with other people to exist.

Let's journey along route number four and follow the compass point of **reflection**.

Reflection is a way to get to know the self.[20] You'll already know that it's the shorthand descriptor for internal self-awareness. This idea of seeing yourself as if in a mirror is commonly used as a metaphor for self-awareness. You want to be able to peer into that mirror with such clarity that you see every pore and blemish, every crease in your shirt. With ordinary human eyes, that's not possible, of course. You don't have 360-degree vision, and you can't see the body language of the people standing beyond your line of sight, staring, or gossiping out of earshot. Sometimes you need to prompt the help of trusted others to help you reflect on your fashion faux pas, language, behaviours and decisions. We'll talk more about the 'how' of reflection in Part 3, but for now, let's talk about the 'why'.

The challenge with reflection is that you have to want to do it, hold a predisposition to do it or have been directed to do it. Introverts have reflection as an in-built 'mechanism of being' and so find it quite natural, which we explored in Part 1. They'll be reflecting moment to moment and actively seeking reflection time before responding or proposing solutions to a problem. In a Threads post in July 2023, Steven Bartlett wrote:

"Creativity is born in silence, mental clarity and solitude. The best ideas come from boredom, not the boardroom."

Music to an introvert's ears.

In his book, *Begin With WE*, Kyle McDowell talks about reflective practice as the 'mirror of truth', right up front on page 22:

"... being overt and purposeful about self-reflection is critically important... I've found if the effort isn't a focussed activity, much-needed introspection tends to be fleeting or simply left undone."

Kyle talks through the way he engages with the mirror of truth on a regular basis. If you're an extrovert, you might want to consider preparing and planning for your reflective practice and thinking about it as being overt and purposeful. This resonates with the whole reason this book overtly and purposefully talks about self-awareness as a superhighway. If you're going about your day-to-day business, you're being carried along by the tide. To develop your self-awareness, you've got to actively manoeuvre onto your elevated superhighway to give yourself the objectivity and perspective you need to actively engage in reflective practice.

The challenge of time is a barrier to being able to be reflective. You most definitely need to carve out time to reflect, whether by giving yourself five minutes to decompress between Zoom meetings or something more substantial like a 60-minute yoga session or 30 minutes walking around your garden smelling the roses. Whatever your situation, you can't reflect if you're too busy to take a breath. One of my top takeaways from my discussion with Neil Jurd (episode 12), author of *The Leadership Book*, was that time out is time well spent. You need to take time to reflect and review. Don't get sucked into doing busy work. Be brave, do nothing and spend time with yourself. Do that one thing you enjoy that's one step away from productive – what a great way to describe an activity. (You know exactly which activity he means, don't you?!). Create space in your brain for the thoughts to come and fill it. Check out Neil's TEDxCroydon talk, 'Pause & Allow', March 2023, where he talks about how controlling less can be the key to success. I was in the audience so heard it first hand!

Reflective practice is talked about quite extensively in relation to healthcare, social care and education. Alison Lagier (episode 7) talked about reflective practice during her time as a student mental health nurse. From the very earliest days of Alison's training, reflective practice was instilled in her as an essential part of delivering good care. Regular clinical supervision was a key component of Alison's training, and her thoughts, beliefs, behaviour and practice were all discussed alongside patient diagnoses and recovery. She said this became a habitual practice that served her well when she moved into management and leadership roles. It became ingrained in her way of working. This is definitely something worth thinking about if you've got a new starter in your organisation and you want your onboarding to establish helpful and enduring reflective practices.

In January 2023, I co-wrote a LinkedIn article with Dr Ketan Kulkarni, physician and co-author of *The Legendary Quest*. We talked about reflective practice in healthcare, particularly nursing care, and how being your 'authentic self' can support therapeutic healing in patients.[21] Have you ever visited a loved one in hospital during illness or recuperation? How did they seem when their favourite helpful, communicative and responsive nurse was on duty? What happened when the doctor who was abrupt, dismissive and rude to their colleagues came along? What was their demeanour then? Now consider the impact this has on healing.

Reflective practice can take many forms, from solo pursuits to interactive activities. The whole of Part 3 is dedicated to sharing methods and tools to develop your self-aware leadership. You will explore things like mindfulness, journaling, coaching and a quiz designed especially for you to accompany this book, the Self-Awareness Compass Quiz.

The fundamental premise of self-aware leadership is that you can't go forward on your superhighway without having looked back and understood the impact you've had on the road behind you. I occasionally got a lift to work with a colleague whose driving was atrocious. I could see other road users dodging out of the way, and I could imagine that, had I looked in the rear-view mirror, I'd have seen cars mounting pavements, vans knocking into lamp posts and pedestrians extricating themselves from the hedges they'd had to jump into. Reflection is essential. Checking what's happened in the rear-view mirror is not an activity to do when you fancy a jolly diversion; it's something you should be doing every few minutes – before you manoeuvre, after you manoeuvre, when you change lane, when you turn off at a junction, when you've cut someone up and when you've parked and turned off the engine. Be that person who knows what's going on in their wake.

5.   Trust

**"Leadership is the relentless pursuit of truth
and ceaseless creation of trust."**
Jack Welch

Trust isn't something you do. Trust is what you instil in others by what you do or don't do. As far as trust is concerned, you can't 'do' trust and you can't 'be' trustworthy simply because you say so or you decide to do a thing you think is worthy of someone else's trust. Trustworthiness is in the eye of the beholder. It's an incredibly important foundational behaviour that underpins all the other CHARTABLE behaviours. You can care for one person and not another, meaning you're not trustworthy.

You can be humble in some situations and not in others, meaning you are neither trustworthy nor authentic. You can model behaviours in your interactions with stakeholders one minute and behave with no integrity as you have an affair in the photocopier room the next, bringing your trustworthiness into question and fraying your reputation. Trust is something that others develop in you by the way you behave and operate and the way you lead the organisation around you. It has no timespan for its creation, but it has a split second in its destruction.

Let's journey along route number five and follow the compass point of **trust**.

You already know that to be self-aware, a leader needs to know themselves well enough to know their own values and beliefs. When they know what they are, they're able to follow their moral compass to present themselves in an authentic and transparent way. This puts them in the best position to be trusted by others – and consistently trusted to the point that they inspire others and people will want to follow them. Leaders who understand and manage their emotions and display self-control act as role models for followers and enhance followers' trust and respect.[22] You don't want a leader who goes into a tailspin and loses their grip in a crisis. That will surely erode trust in a heartbeat. Being vulnerable and humble are not behaviours that demonstrate leaders as being out of control, but rather leaders who are confident, honest and want to learn how to make things better.

A *Harvard Business Review* article, 'How to Build Trust at Work: Our Favorite Reads' by Kelsey Alpaio shares a number of different ways that trust is demonstrated by others:

> **"It may seem like a mushy word, but it can show up in some really concrete ways. When your boss gives you the opportunity to lead a new project without looking over your shoulder — that's trust. When your organization's executives are open and honest about the challenges the company is facing — that's trust. And when your direct reports respect your ideas and decisions, but still feel able to challenge you when needed — that's trust too."**

In June 2023, there was an article in *The Times of India* titled 'Learn to trust your team, don't be a micro-manager' written by Tarun Rai, a veteran of 35 years in the sales, marketing and then advertising and media worlds. In describing trust, he says, "Don't be a micro-manager. Learn to trust your team. Only then can you delegate effectively. Give your team the freedom to fail." This is another example of describing things by both setting out what they are as well as what they aren't.

When I spoke to leadership strategist and culture change expert Dan Pontefract (episode 29), I asked him about trust, as it's one of the work factors he sets out in his book *Work-Life BLOOM*. He described trust as having three pillars: authenticity, advocacy and consistency. Being authentic means not donning a Teflon suit and not spouting fake news. Advocacy is believing in and backing up your team, even when they're not in the room. Consistency is operating within a bandwidth of emotional highs and lows – being unpredictable, inconsistent and erratic means people don't know where they stand with you.

If you want a reputation for being a self-aware leader, you have to live and breathe the nine CHARTABLE self-aware leadership behaviours, even if some of them aren't things you can actively do, like trust, but merely hope to achieve by means of other behaviours. If you want to be authentic as a leader, you tell the truth and are trusted; you do what you say you're going to do.[23] Doing what you say you'll do develops your reputation for being trustworthy, authentic and having integrity. But, like so many other things in life, it's when you don't deliver on your commitments that things get tricky.

If you say you're going to do something for someone and then you don't, their perception will be either that you forgot because you didn't care enough to remember or you had something better to do. Either way, by not sticking to your word, you've let them down, and now they don't know if they can trust you to have their back in the future. They'll have to work around you and put back-up plans in place just in case you don't deliver on the goods.

Matt Stone (episode 10) said whether you're talking about a marriage or a business relationship, there are commonalities to making a relationship good. Trust is at the core of relationships, and all kinds of relationships need trust to be effective. Building trust also means building your personal brand and your reputation.

I'm reminded of a colleague, who had been acting up in a senior role, being interviewed for the substantive job. They didn't get it and a ripple went through the department: "They were robbed!", "Pah, good enough to do the job when no one else would do it, but not good enough for the title now, are they?!" This was the same colleague who, in an organisation-wide meeting a year or two before, had admitted to a breakout group I was in that they'd been caught by the police joyriding when they were about 17. I remembered the little voice in my head saying, "Too much informaaaaaaaation!!!" I was later told by a reliable source that they didn't get the job because they weren't polished enough and, in an instant, I knew exactly what they meant. The person was a bit of a 'Jack the lad', albeit bright, quick-witted and not one to suffer fools gladly. But yes, they didn't have that polish, and I could see exactly why the suited majority didn't want that kind of person rubbing shoulders with them at the boardroom table. When your reputation precedes you, it doesn't matter what your interview scores are; they will add up to the 'right' number in the end... If you haven't built up a reputation where people are certain you're not going to out yourself, them or the organisation, then you won't have the trust of your colleagues. If you've pissed off the wrong people, they're not going to do right by you.

Being that trust isn't one thing but rather a collection of things, it's often described in the negative because it's often easier to describe what something isn't than what it is! Things like arrogance, aloofness, perfectionism, insensitivity, selfishness and detachment[24] all put you in the untrustworthy category. Leaders who are self-deceiving and have a warped view of reality are more prone to overlook their duty to others and are then viewed as untrustworthy by colleagues. This leads to faith in them as individuals, and their organisation as a whole, being undermined.[25]

Psychological safety is underpinned by trust. You need to trust that you can challenge your manager's decision and not be penalised for it. You need to trust that you can raise relationship difficulties with your colleagues without repercussions. You need to trust that if you give feedback to your peers, they're not going to take umbrage and ostracise you from the group. You need to trust that your manager's not going to throw you under the bus or stab you in the back.

Because trust is such a difficult concept to pin down and means different things to different people, I posted a poll on LinkedIn in August 2023 asking the question, 'What is the best way for leaders to inspire trust?' These are the responses I got:

- **Keep promises - 29%**
- **Make difficult decisions - 0%**
- **Admit mistakes - 53%**
- **Other - 18%**

This little bit of research suggested to me that humility is one of the best ways of generating trust, closely followed by integrity.

In my discussion with anti-bullying expert Nicki Eyre and Jonathan Wilson, an ex-senior police officer with personal experience of workplace bullying (episode 28), we explored bullying and harassment, which erode trust, hindering communication and collaboration. When people don't trust each other, they're less likely to express concerns or seek help. When leaders are accountable and hold others accountable for actions, decisions and behaviour, it reinforces trust in an organisation.

To be able to determine how to build trust in your team, you need to know who the authentic work-you is and operate with consistency and integrity in the discharge of your duties. You also need to know your colleagues and teams well enough to know what they need from you as a leader and be able to respond to that honestly and candidly. Being able to visualise and conceptualise the reputation you want to have in the eyes of others will help you formulate an operating model for yourself that is underpinned by being trustworthy.

6.   Adaptability

**"Everyone thinks of changing the world,
but no one thinks of changing himself."**
Leo Tolstoy

Covid took adaptability to a whole new level! The kind of adaptation foisted on organisations during the pandemic meant adoption and implementation of the concept of adaptability en masse. Something not seen in the lifetime of most of us (albeit, I wouldn't want to tempt fate and suggest it isn't something we won't see again...). In 2018 BC (before Covid), when people talked about adaptability, it was more related to occasionally working from home and the odd maverick company offering it as the norm, not the exception. It was about technical radicals using video conferencing regularly, rather than the rest of us who used it once in a blue moon and generally gave up because the cables didn't fit. Now, adaptability is an essential behaviour for the 21st-century post-pandemic working world of the enlightened.

Let's journey along route number six and follow the compass point of **adaptability**.

When you're exploring adaptability, it's helpful to group your thoughts into adaptability of systems, organisations and individuals. Let's consider the macro, meso and micro levels of adaptability that people operate in. But let's be clear: they're all influenced and impacted by people, so the reference to organisations doesn't abrogate the responsibility of leaders within them. Too often we talk about organisations as if they were independent organic entities, but they're not. They're a collection of people where leaders make the decisions, drive the priorities, set the standards and create the culture. When we talk about these three layers of adaptability, we're simply giving shorthand terms to the people who make up each layer.

We dived into complex adaptive systems in Chapter 4 when we explored leadership at all levels. A complex adaptive system considers how different people operate within a system or organisation, not necessarily linked to hierarchy. We also swam around in complexity leadership, which considers the needs of projects and sees leadership moving to different people within the system who have the right skills at the right time to deliver the project. This means that the leadership function is movable, flexible and adaptable. There's a dichotomy, though. The vast majority of people work in organisations with a traditional triangular-shaped structure, with fewer people at the top and more people at the bottom, as you discovered in the section about leaders with titles and leaders without. This means there are different power dynamics going on in the organisation at the same time: the 'because it's in my job description and this is what I'm paid to do' dynamic alongside the 'you're the best person to lead this project because you have the skills we need right now' dynamic. It seems that adaptive systems are alive and well in organisations regardless of hierarchy and the red tape of bureaucracy (more on that later).

Adaptive leadership focusses on harnessing new discoveries, innovation and problem solving as a means of adapting to change. In the most complex environments, "adaptive practices predominate".[26] This idea was out in the world in 2017, before Covid was even a wriggle in a Petri dish.

When you're considering the actual function of leadership in the knowledge-based paradigm and thinking about how traditional structures operate alongside adaptive systems, you also need to think about hybrid working and delegation. They are two very practical and visible ways that you see adaptability playing out at the macro, meso and micro levels – or not, as the case may be!

Jacqui Frost (episode 9) said when leaders know themselves well enough to know what they don't know and are able to delegate effectively to someone who does, that demonstrates they have a pretty good level of self-awareness. They also have the confidence to be vulnerable enough to say, "Someone needs to help me do this thing." If you behave in such a way that makes people think you know it all and model that by taking on all of the problem solving and the fixing, all it serves to do is de-skill and disempower people around you. That then puts you in the position of having to have all the answers and make all the decisions about everything. You've backed yourself into a corner or pushed yourself so far up the pyramid of hierarchy that you can't get down. This is not adaptability; this isn't showing responsiveness and flexibility. It isn't showing trust and faith in others' abilities either. This is fixed and needs some tender loving care to oil the gears and get the machine moving again.

A big part of leadership is knowing when to get out of the way – that's how Neil Jurd (episode 12) puts it. The trouble with delegation is that it keeps the leader's brain in every learning loop. Leaders need to build the skills, confidence and competence of their team to allow them to get on with the work without the leader's involvement. Leaders need to upskill, develop and nurture innovation in their teams and then let them get on with it. Leaders need to harness the brilliance of people around them and then get out of their way. This is adaptability – where you draw on the right strengths of the right people at the right time to deliver the job at hand.

Pastor and founder of the American evangelical church Life Church Craig Groeschel says, "If you delegate tasks, you create followers. If you delegate authority, you create leaders." As the problems of the working world, and arguably the planet, become more complex, empowerment of others is increasingly important. If you don't, the next cohort of microbiologists, virologists and epidemiologists who you're going to need to step onto that stage is not going to be primed to pivot, flex and adapt to the ensuing catastrophe. Researchers of a 2014 study discovered that the competencies that would be valued in the future would be adaptability, self-awareness, boundary spanning, collaboration and network thinking.[27] Little did they know.

Ira Wolfe (episode 24), a future-of-work global thought leader and founder of the Googlization Nation community, talked to me about the adapt-abilities: the abilities required for adaptation. They are grit, resilience, mental flexibility, unlearning and growth mindset. Unlearning was a major factor in adaptability, and Ira talked about this on Penny Zenker's *Take Back Time* podcast in June 2021 too, describing unlearning as 'defragging your brain'. If you had a PC in the noughties, you probably defragged your hard disc from time to time. This, Ira said, is what you need to do with all the things you've learnt and stored in your brain. For adaptability, you need to learn to unlearn the knowledge and skills you've acquired because 'what got you here might not get you there' (thanks to Dr Marshall Goldsmith, the number one executive coach as rated by Thinkers50, for that fitting phrase!).

Being adaptable is a prerequisite for self-awareness. If you are self-aware and want to regulate your behaviour in response to what you're experiencing and observing, you need to be adaptable and flexible. Amy Gandon (episode 15), a policy professional and author of the *Civil unrest* report, said that being agile is important in our future-focussed, climate-conscious workplaces. To be agile, compassionate and empathetic, you need to be self-aware so you can tap into your hard skills and relational skills to deal with the challenges ahead. The Global Talent Trends (LinkedIn Talent Solutions, 2019) study carried out by LinkedIn, which surveyed over 5,000 talent professionals and considered behavioural data and activity on LinkedIn, identified soft skills as the top trend relevant to the future workplace, listing the top five soft skills as creativity, persuasion, collaboration, adaptability and time management. The updated report, released in May 2023, found that employees' top values were compensation, work–life balance and flexibility in working arrangements. With both adaptability and flexibility featuring in the reports published either side of Covid, it suggests the demand for greater adaptability was gaining pace and was just accelerated by Covid. Organisational leaders need to be adaptable if they want to retain good people and survive into the 2030s and beyond.

As an individual, embracing change is not easy. Over the last 20 years, change in organisations has been accelerating. In the public sector, people with the job titles of 'change agent' and 'transformation manager' used to be dotted around organisations like map pins, but with change and transformation becoming more of a business-as-usual function and everybody involved in some kind of change or transformation at one time or other in their role, there is far less need for dedicated jobs now. What that does mean, though, is individuals who have a fixed mindset are less able and prepared to put their pedal to the metal and accelerate out of the chicane than those with a growth mindset, putting the less adaptable at a discernible disadvantage in the future career market.

Doing something new is easy; doing something you've done before in a different way is not so easy. People with a growth mindset will definitely embrace this challenge in a way that the fixed-mindsetters won't. The fixed-mindsetters will be struggling with the recollection of effort and learning they had to go through to get them to where they are and will be concerned that doing something differently next time means that everything they've worked so hard for was worth nothing or is useless for the modern age. But let's hang on a second. Let's not overthink this.

Everything you learnt yesterday and last month and over the last 20 years means you have hard skills and relational skills that are transferable to the here and now. You've been to that job interview that asked about your transferable skills, haven't you? Well, that's what this is, but instead of being a 45-minute interview, it's an all-day every-day thing. Everything you've done and every skill you've acquired has taught you how to learn, and if you can learn, you can unlearn and re-learn. That's what makes you adaptable. Adaptability doesn't have to be about going from zero to hero in a split second; it's about keeping up with the flow of traffic, pre-empting what's coming up around the bend and being ready to power out of the corner to grab on to new experiences. It's about being welcoming of new ideas and being excited about what's coming up over the horizon.

7.   Behaviour

"Setting an example is not the main means of influencing others; it is the only means."
Albert Einstein

Behaviour. It's a huge topic. It's everything you do, everything you say, every move you make, every decision you take (see Chapter 1!). When you consider behaviour from the perspective of self-aware leadership, you're talking about deliberate behaviour: behaving from a place of knowing, choosing and pre-empting the consequences. It's a conscious behaviour. It's responding, not reacting. From my research, I was able to identify three particular elements of behaviour that were relevant to self-awareness: situational behaviour, modelling behaviour and unethical behaviour.

Let's journey along route number seven and follow the compass point of **behaviour**.

To influence the responses you get in different situations, you need to be able to regulate your behaviour. And to do that, you need to be aware of it. You need to know your audience to be able to decide how you need to behave. Situational behaviour means observing your hard and relational skills, recognising your impact and regulating your behaviour, all in the moment, and then pivoting to a different behaviour in the next situation.

Then there's modelling behaviour – which is by far the greatest topic of conversation of all the elements of behaviour. Modelling behaviour is a fundamental consideration for a self-aware leader. As you saw earlier, every move you make is observed, scrutinised and sends a signal to people right across the organisation about what is acceptable, what is tolerated and what is good. One of my research interviewees said, "My current manager lacks any self-awareness and certainly doesn't demonstrate leadership, right down to rarely being present in the office and then being surprised when others model that behaviour." Colleagues pick up on the principles of a leader's behaviour and implement those behaviours in their contexts. It becomes a framework of acceptable behaviour. If you read your phone in a one-to-one meeting with your direct report, they'll think it's okay to take their phone into a meeting with their team.

I once had a senior manager who used to stop by my office from time to time. One day, they'd arranged to pop in for a catch-up to see how things were going. They sat in the low-slung chair I had and checked their phone whilst I was speaking. I stopped speaking for a moment or two, as I was already aware of the neuroscience of multi-tasking (i.e. it's not possible; it's simply adeptness at task-switching), and they said, "It's okay, I am listening." I said something like, "No, that's okay. I'll wait for you to finish," but they insisted. I begrudgingly carried on, feeling like second best and annoyed that I was having to give up my time and energy to be wholly present to speak to them (I mean, they were the senior manager) whilst they were only giving me part of their attention. Still, I learnt what type of leader I didn't want to be that day, so I guess it wasn't all bad.

Robertson Hunter Stewart (episode 8) gave an example of one of his managers shouting at an employee for not being nice to customers. The manager hadn't spotted that taking a disrespectful, public and very negative approach to try and elicit a positive behaviour from the member of staff was a little ironic. The manager didn't have awareness of his wider impact beyond his bubble of red mist. The moral of Robertson's story? If you want staff to be nicer to customers, be nicer to your staff!

In podcast episode 22, Dr Gerrit Pelzer referenced his model of 'perception management', which is a sibling to my description of 'regulation'. He talked about Armin Laschet, who campaigned to be the next chancellor of Germany following Angela Merkel's departure in 2021. Laschet had visited a flooding site during his campaign phase and had been caught laughing in the background of a video. If you search for it on Google, you'll get a raft of results about 'laughing Laschet'. As you might expect, the pretender to the throne was knocked out of the running.

Think about your own behaviour. You might be responding to a situation within your close sphere of proximity, but your behaviour might be perceived very differently by those observing you from a distance. Your leadership shadow extends much further than the distance of a private joke!

In my research questionnaire and interviews, people frequently talked about poor behaviour, sharing examples like promotion by longevity or circumstance rather than ability or effective leadership (which was felt to be more of a thing for men, i.e. the 'old boys' network'), using position or rank as a lever to 'get what they want' and justify decisions made. I remember once hearing about someone who was being put forward for a pay rise. It wasn't your run-of-the-mill £1,200; it was about £10,000. Because of the amount, it had to go to the organisation's most senior public committee for approval. The individual was already in a bit of an awkward position, as their parent was a senior figure in the community, and the talk was that they'd only got the job because something was whispered into the right ear. Once the committee papers were out in the public domain, the outcry began and gradually became louder until eventually the paper was withdrawn. After the brouhaha died down, I was chewing the cud with one of those colleagues that sees all, hears all and rarely says very much, and they told me that 'Tricky Dicky' played golf at the same club as the CEO. What a coincidence! Clearly promotions happen on the golf courses I don't frequent rather than the ice-cream parlours I do. You too, huh?

One of my interviewees shared an experience of a manager using personal details following a 360-degree review against subordinates. Poor behaviour was described as manipulative and divisive, and it was said that certain individuals would "trample on the people who care".

There are a number of behaviours that form barriers to developing positive working relationships through a lack of self-awareness, like defensiveness, over-controlling tendencies, insensitivity, abrasiveness, being too assertive, coldness and arrogance, alienating subordinates, unbridled self-interest, micromanagement and defensiveness.[28] As I'm writing this list, I'm allocating the names of the colleagues I've worked with who've demonstrated these behaviours. And you??

Of course, it's not just how you behave that's under the magnifying glass. "The culture of an organisation is shaped by the worst behaviour the leader is willing to tolerate," said Dr Todd Whitaker, a professor in educational leadership. I'm with Todd.

The behaviour you deny as a leader is significant. I use the word 'deny' purposely here. On the continuum between positive and negative, it's one of the most damaging leadership behaviours, with the likes of mentor, nurture, encourage over on one side of the spectrum and tolerate, suppress and deny on the other.

There are numerous organisations where reprehensible behaviour has been exhibited or tolerated by the leaders. Others have found themselves complicit because they copied the boss, didn't prevent what the boss also didn't prevent, or let the boss get away with doing stuff. Reports like the Baroness Casey Review into the standards of behaviour and internal culture of the Metropolitan Police Service in the UK list a failure of leadership and describe suppression tactics as instrumental in not stamping out misogyny and racial and sexual discrimination. The poorest behaviour you accept will be the standard people will rise (or fall) to.

"Your life, career and relationships will rise or fall to the level of the standards you defend, enforce and accept. Raise your bar."
Steven Bartlett

You may have spotted that I've used the words 'boss' and 'leader' interchangeably above. I've done that to stress the point. I've already talked about titled leaders and social leaders and how the terms are used interchangeably but actually mean different things. Managers, bosses, leaders – they're not the same thing, but we tend to use them around the watercooler as if they are.

"The world is changed by your example, not by your opinion."
Paulo Coelho

In April 2023, I replied to a post on LinkedIn that shared this quote, saying, "Definitely. That's why modelling behaviour is essential for effective leadership!" and a guy who referred to himself as a 'Consultant, Superintendent, Author/Speaker', who talked about education, leadership, growth mindset, entrepreneurship and 21st-century skills, responded with "Are you your employees' parent now? Modelling behaviour? What kind of behaviour are you modelling??" I was just a little curious about his knowledge of sociology, groupthink and crowd dynamics, particularly being that his profile said he'd written books about education in schools! I'm interested to know what you think. You can connect with me on social media and share your thoughts. Pop to The Back Pages for contact information.

When you talk about displaying behaviours, you can't but connect it with the idea of emotional contagion. Emotions are contagious. You'll have seen as many YouTube videos as I have where one person starts laughing and eventually the whole train carriage is laughing. There's the guy who starts dancing on the hill and eventually the whole hill is bouncing with dancing people. If emotions are contagious, then so are attitudes, behaviours and all other relational acts and omissions. If humans have a propensity to follow the crowd and the leader of that crowd pays your wages, you can bet we're going to follow them. Leaders lead by example and employees follow that example.

"The world is changed by your example, not by your opinion."

Paulo Coelho

If you want to be an effective self-aware leader, then your behaviour and the behaviour of others matters. A lot. In February 2023, I listened to a brilliant episode of the *Manager Tools Podcast* called 'Culture Chapter 1 - Culture Is Behavior'. They set it out simply and succinctly: culture is formed by the behaviour that goes on in your organisation. That's it. Whatever's written in the corporate strategy about values, forget it. That's just paper. Behaviour is the practice, and together, the behaviour in practice equals the culture of your organisation. I hate conflict and having difficult conversations about awkward things, but I will do it because the alternative is that I let bad behaviour continue making other people's work lives suck. And that, I won't stand for. Will you?

8.   Listening

"Knowledge speaks, but wisdom listens."
Jimi Hendrix

Being ignored, being marginalised, not valued, bypassed, just a number. What's your name again? You have to listen to understand, and you have to listen to respond too. The meme that does the rounds every so often saying, "You should listen to understand, not to respond" doesn't feel realistic to me. Of course you have to respond and, particularly as leaders, you're often expected to have most if not all the answers ready to share. Your humility gives you the opportunity to say, "I don't know," but that doesn't mean it's always a satisfactory response to unhappy people. How then do you put those two things together to ensure you both hear the voices of your colleagues and employees and are able to respond in real time, or at least within a reasonable time?

Let's journey along route number eight and follow the compass point of **listening**.

I used to go to a regular meeting made up of about 30 or so attendees, and in that meeting, there were three or four voices that would dominate the discussion. No matter who chaired the meeting, they couldn't control the amount of airspace these people consumed. Their voices were so loud in the room that most of them, at one time or another, had been voted into the role of the chair in the hope they would either be quieter or take up the whole of the agenda and give us all a day off with a free lunch. A day or two before the meeting, I would often check who was attending and who had sent apologies. If any of the loud few were in attendance, I'd feign an illness or an urgent matter that needed to be dealt with as often as I could without being conspicuous by my absence. The inability to create listening space to hear the voices of others was jaw-dropping. The eye rolling, yawning and email answering that went on in that room on those days made it a very expensive waiting room!

Active listening is an essential function of leadership. It's a critical mechanism for getting to know yourself better through the eyes of others (recognition) and giving yourself the best opportunity to behave in the way you would most want in any situation (regulation). It also ensures people feel heard and are heard. If you think about the recognition layer of self-aware leadership, it's about using all the senses you have at your disposal to take in what another person is communicating. I should clarify, when we talk about listening in this book, it's listening to what's being said, how it's being said and what's not being said and 'listening' to what's being subconsciously conveyed too. This compass point includes inter-relational communication in all its guises: verbal, non-verbal and visual. As a self-aware leader, you need to listen to what's being said, how it's being said and the harmony or dissonance between the two.

As a leader, you need to create listening environments. You've already read about extroverts and introverts and how difficult it is for introverts to find that space in the conversation to raise their voice. Your job as a leader is to create those spaces and opportunities. Virtual meetings are good for generating these opportunities. Everyone being in a little virtual square is a pretty good leveller, provided the rule of engagement is that people use their little yellow hand to make a point. I talked to coach for introverts and quiet achievers Serena Low (episode 46) about this. She said extroverts can dominate virtual discussions too and don't always use their little yellow hand! This means the role of the discussion facilitator is to lay out the ground rules to ensure listening is set as one of the operating standards of the session and there are opportunities for quieter voices to be heard.

I struggle not to talk over the end of people's sentences. Apparently this is a common trait of introverts, as we're not very good at jumping in before the extroverts and then misjudge when someone else has finished speaking. I do my best to write down my thoughts and bring them up when the conversation has ended, but I don't always manage it and I'm not always guaranteed to get my two penn'orth in before the louder voices. I do, however, own my faux pas and you'll often hear me saying, "Sorry, I cut across you there" as a way of living my compass points of care, humility, authenticity, reflection and modelling behaviour.

I recently did two podcast interviews where I'd asked my guests a really good question, and as they were answering, I threw in a side comment. They totally lost their thread, and I totally forgot what I'd asked them. I was listening to work out what I could ask them next so that the podcast could be engaging, relevant and had flow. This is my greatest challenge – listening whilst holding on to a comment related to something someone said earlier for long enough so that I can come in and make it. I've usually forgotten it by the time I get the chance, and you've missed the benefit of my wit and wisdom!! Listening, hearing and responding are tough skills to master!

I heard Oscar Trimboli, an expert in listening and the author of *Deep Listening*, talking to Jon Rennie on the *Deep Leadership* podcast. His website is a treasure trove of useful resources for listeners and people who want to improve their listening. He sets out five layers of listening: listening to yourself, listening to the content, listening to the context, listening to the unsaid and listening for meaning. There's a quiz on Oscar's website that "will help you identify your Listening Villains, and provide you with a clear understanding of your number one listening barrier". I took it, being that I have an interest in self-awareness, don'tcha know, and my listening villain is 'The Shrewd Listener'...

> **"Savvy thinker – fixing fixated – three steps ahead of the wrong problem. Shrewd Listeners are obsessed with solutions rather than listening. You are too busy trying to solve the issue before you have properly listened to the situation and explanation."**

Don't you just hate it when these things are right? Take the test, I dare you!

I liked what Jon Rennie (episode 11) said about the need to listen to everybody. He said, as leaders, we should cultivate our complainers because they might just be trying to make things better. Some people who complain do so from a place of genuine concern, and their concern has built up to a grievance through frustration because no one was listening. When you think about the complainers, a self-aware leader needs to separate out what's being said from how it's being said. If you're dealing with someone who's been labelled a complainer, it might be that how they're raising a challenge is simply rubbing people up the wrong way. If you take the how out of the what, it might be that the substance of what they're trying to say is valuable and important to the existence of your company. As Jon said, if you're a leader, you've really got to develop a thick skin and learn to be open to the complainers. Different people convey their emotions in different ways, and some people may not fall within your experience of atypical emotional displays. Listen to your complainers, and maybe, just maybe, they'll be throwing you a lifeline that you didn't know you needed!

When I talked to Alison Smith (episode 4), she spoke about communication and said, what you give out, you get back: the meaning of the communication is the response you get, which is quite a humbling thought. If people receive what you're saying in a way that you didn't intend, consider that it's unlikely to be their fault. Did you communicate appropriately for your audience? Being that 'you can't change others, you can only change yourself', consider the things within your locus of control and listen to the responses you're getting. If they don't align, change what you're saying.

A *Harvard Business Review* article titled 'What Great Listeners Actually Do' by Jack Zenger and Joseph Folkman sets out what great listeners actually do: they ask questions that promote discovery and insight, have interactions that build self-esteem and create a safe environment, have co-operative conversations where feedback flows both ways; they make suggestions skilfully and open up alternative paths to thinking and problem solving.

They also describe six levels of listening:

1. Create a safe environment to discuss.
2. Clear away distractions and make eye contact.
3. Understand the substance, ask questions and confirm.
4. Observe non-verbal clues.
5. Understand emotions and feelings about the topic.
6. Help other people to see issues in a different light.

These are incredibly helpful steps along a journey to improved and active listening.

To listen better, you need to work on your own active listening skills. To hear better, you need to work on your organisation's hearing mechanisms. If you want to operate as an effective self-aware listening leader, you need to consider the environment, methods, standards and opportunities for your colleagues to be engaged and feel safe enough to speak, write and indicate in whatever way is most appropriate to them, their thoughts, ideas and views.

9.   Experience

"I never lose. I either win or learn."
Nelson Mandela

Intertwined with humility and reflection is learning from experience and sharing experiences. Fundamental to the onward journey of self-aware leadership is learning – your own and that of others. We've already set out the argument that leadership is not a skill that can be learnt, like a technical skill; there must first be an innate ability that is cultivated, nurtured and developed through learning. And what better way to learn than by experience? As a leader determined to develop your hard and relational self-awareness skills, it's your responsibility to seek out exposure to learning opportunities. Likewise, it's incumbent on you to pass on those opportunities for experiential learning to others. You need to strive forward on your journey, push through the hurricanes, battle through the storms and hunker down in the typhoons because you will, without a shadow of a doubt, become a better version of yourself for having learnt from experience – what you would do bigger, better, faster, more of… next time.

Let's journey along route number nine and follow the final compass point on your journey of self-aware leadership: **experience**.

The Leadership Behaviours Framework for Senior Leaders, developed by Academi Wales (the leadership and management development body for the Welsh public sector),[29] identifies the core leadership behaviours of learning, self-awareness, drive and resilience. As core leadership behaviours, learning and self-awareness are described as the capacity for learning from experience and feedback and adapting one's approach to take account of that learning and feedback. Academi Wales is of the view that learning and self-awareness matter because they support a leader to grow, improve, reduce repeated mistakes and facilitate other behaviours necessary for high-level performance.

Experience is considered an element of self-awareness.[30] The experience you gain from leading in a crisis means you can use it to mould your leadership styles and learn how to improve for the future[31] because "leadership is hardwired through the experience of adversity". As Confucius says, it is one of the ways to learn wisdom. When you've engaged in a social or collaborative learning experience, the knowledge and skills you acquire become neurologically embedded and stick better in your brain.[32]

In general terms, you 'know' your world through your experiences, and your experiences are individual to you. There are, of course, instances where you know a rock is heavy and a car is fast because of the weights, measurements and speeds set out for you by science. But excluding all the things that are solid, tangible and quantifiable, everything else is a story. You know that if you have two people in a room, both will leave remembering the same, similar and different things. If 20 people watch the Tour de France, you'll get 20 differing accounts. When my husband

and I go out to a restaurant, I'll be able to describe the décor, where the other diners sat, what they wore and how they behaved towards each other. My husband will recall who said what to whom and the details of the menu. Neither of us will be able to recall the same thing as the other.

You experience the world in relation to others by the stories you tell yourself and the ones told to you by others. You perceive your world through the senses you have available to you, your natural dispositions to observe certain things, your different interests, your biases, your culture, your religion and what you've learnt from your parents, families, communities and past experiences. Assistant fire chief Chad Costa (episode 23) said that life experiences like marriage and having children change you. You can add illness, bereavement, divorce and house moves to that list. The experiences that impact and change you influence the way you see and experience the world and the stories you tell yourself and others about it. You live, rocks and cars aside, in a socially constructed world.

This idea of lived experience connects to the discussion in Part 1 about nature versus nurture and whether it's really possible to learn leadership. As you've read, this book takes the stance that leadership can't be learnt without either some evident or undiscovered leadership attributes being innately present. You can, however, build on the innate capabilities you have, through formal learning and experiential learning.

You generally learn from experiencing things via the indirect stories of others or by directly experiencing things yourself. Putting in place opportunities to experience and learn from others through mentoring, supervision, masterclasses and training are positive ways to hear the stories and learn from others through indirect experiences. These are helpful for individuals recently promoted to leadership and management positions or people new to their roles because they provide supplementary learning experiences that can be tapped into whilst doing the day job.

Direct experiences can also be sought out. Shadowing, internships, volunteering, on-the-job learning courses, promotion, interim roles or doing roles at the cusp of your circle of knowledge are all ways to instigate direct learning opportunities. These lend themselves to situations where you're more ready and able to relinquish your substantive role, either wholly or partially, permanently or temporarily.

Within organisations, the sharing of experiences is generally through internal and external communication, and communication here is meant in its very broadest sense – for example, the language and vocabulary that's used and the nuances given in corporate messaging, like how reports are written, whether the history of the organisation is talked about, what social media communications are put out into the world and the tone of the leadership and management courses endorsed by the organisation.

One of the underpinning skills of internal and external communication is storytelling. The benefits of storytelling are widely acknowledged. Storytelling is also about evidencing the impact of your efforts. Storytelling as a business skill has been gaining momentum over the last 15 years (in the public sector in the UK, at least) alongside the embracing of results-based accountability and the use of qualitative and outcomes measures. If you want to be able to determine the outcome of your work, you have to be able to tell the qualitative story and justify your financial investment by proving that someone was better off after your efforts than before. You're already adept at telling the quantitative story, but telling the qualitative story is a work in progress. You need to be able to share your work experiences and the impact they're having on others to be able to justify the continuation of your job. If you can't set out a story of impact, why would anyone want to continue employing you? In your organisation, this might fall under the banner of productivity.

There are examples of managers preparing staff at operational and business levels for promotion because they've seen potential in those individuals. You can encourage people to find external coaches and mentors, organise shadowing opportunities, give people chances to step up into temporary promotion positions, ask them to attend senior meetings to present papers and get their names on the radar. Also consider this in instances where individuals don't have the level of confidence in themselves that you have in them – where you're able to see their potential as strategic thinkers, integration and engagement experts and leaders well before they can.

When you consider people in your organisation who show potential and innate leadership capabilities, they will benefit greatly from training and increased exposure to experiential learning opportunities. And the organisation will benefit alongside them. In many cases though, organisations let good talent go to build their experiences elsewhere, and hope they'll come back one day when they've built up those skills.

There's definitely an argument for supporting people to gain a broad range of experiences in different roles, within different organisations and sectors, but this has to be weighed up against the unintended consequences of creating a churn of people joining and leaving organisations. More work needs to be done in terms of developing case studies and facilitating storytelling as a means of nurturing individuals working their way up the career ladder so that they stay a bit longer, create a bit more stability within organisations and then move on in a planned way, not a running-for-the-hills kind of way because the organisation doesn't nurture them to grow in knowledge and skills.

As a self-aware leader on their journey of improvement, you need to suck every drop of learning from your experiences. And when you've done that, as a caring, humble, relationship-focussed leader, you need to create a tsunami of sharing with your colleagues to foster an organisational culture of learning, failing and learning again, underpinned by the psychological safety, confidence, trust and back-up to do so.

In the Rear-View Mirror

You came to the roundabout and you didn't know which road you should take. Now you know about the journey along the superhighway in each of the nine directions. You know which direction each road will take you...

If you take the superhighway of CARE, you are heading on a journey of empathy and respect, appreciating the human aspects of the lives of your colleagues whilst not shying away from having difficult conversations.

If you take the superhighway of HUMILITY, your sojourn will be filled with letting others' light shine, supporting them to step forward and being open when you don't know the answers.

If you take the superhighway of AUTHENTICITY, your hike will show you how to live your values, beliefs and priorities with integrity and make conscious decisions about who the professional 'you' really is.

If you take the superhighway of REFLECTION, your cruise will involve being reflective in the moment and giving yourself the opportunity to respond rather than react so you can grow and become the best version of yourself.

If you take the superhighway of TRUST, you'll trek into the land of kindness and consistency where you will instil trust in your colleagues so that they choose to follow you.

If you take the superhighway of ADAPTABILITY, your expedition will mean responding with openness, flexibility and a growth mindset to the changing demands of your role and the changing needs of your people.

If you take the superhighway of BEHAVIOUR, your ride will mean modelling the behaviour you expect to see in your organisation and rewarding the behaviour of those that live the values you espouse.

If you take the superhighway of LISTENING, you are heading on a voyage of giving voice to the quieter and marginalised people in your organisations to ensure everyone is heard.

If you take the superhighway of EXPERIENCE, your flight will mean learning from your experiences and sharing what you know with others to nurture their growth and development.

The tools I share with you in Part 3 will help you decide which route to take, which roads you already know better than you think and which pathways are most unfamiliar. But for now, let's journey on to explore the signposts and directions that will enable your journey of self-aware leadership and the roadblocks and trip hazards that will obstruct you.

6. SIGNPOSTS AND DIRECTIONS

Chapter Map

Self-aware leadership is a socially constructed concept, meaning it can only happen when you're in relation to other people. Introspection alone is merely internal self-awareness, and leadership in an empty room is self-mastery. To know yourself, you need others, and when you're in organisations with others, they and you need signposts and directions to guide you towards self-awareness.

You're going to travel through the organisational enablers of self-aware leadership, starting with strategy and planning. You'll then take a right turn and head on to organisational standards. Then the landscape changes as you move into the ocean of people management and explore recruitment, supervision and performance reviews, organisational development and wellbeing. Next, you'll head inland, leaving the choppy seas of people management behind you as you discover teams, peers, communities and inclusive decision making.

Let's roll the windows down, turn the music up and head into the light.

Strategy and Planning

Strategy development and business planning are generally viewed as inconveniences that detract people from their work and things people have to do on top of their day job. Very few organisations or teams have cracked the code to enable people to do strategy and planning as part of their work. Maybe because it's not something you do every day, maybe because it's not something that involves everyone all of the time, maybe because it's sometimes abstract and people feel they can't contribute. Maybe it's all of those things. It's difficult to pin down why strategy and planning are so poorly promoted and badly received. But you only realise the importance of strategy when it's not there and the importance of a plan when no one knows where they're going.

A strategy sets the direction for every single thing that happens in an organisation, from the hard things to the relational things. It's an organisational guide map for priorities and areas of focus. It sets out values and principles against which all work life should be lived – what an organisation is going to do and what it isn't. If you can't make the connection between the thing you're doing at work right now and your organisational strategy, there's a pretty strong argument that you shouldn't be doing that thing.

Am I evangelising? You betcha.

As you move into roles with greater responsibility and leadership expectations, being able to see the strategy and the bigger picture will become necessary. Knowing there is a level of detailed implementation underneath the strategic objectives, and a set of detailed actions under that, will become increasingly important to you as you move up the career ladder.

I had a conversation with strategy expert Jeroen Kraaijenbrink (episode 16). Jeroen said strategy is about relationships, both in terms of developing strategy and implementing it. Strategy only works if it's a participative activity, meaning that strategy relies on relationships and, as you know, relationships rely on self-awareness. There needs to be organisational awareness of vision, mission and principles, along with individuals' self-awareness of their behaviour in building relationships for strategy development and implementation. The social engagement you create through the strategy development process is very important. When you have clarity of direction, you can work out what skills you need in your organisation to effectively reach your goals. With awareness of the self and awareness of others, you can build a team that works towards that direction.

If you want to develop effective working relationships and capitalise on what increasing self-aware leadership can achieve, you need to establish it from your strategy: the thing that gives life, soul and aspirations to your organisation. Then you have to bring your strategy to life through the behaviours that are encouraged, celebrated and rewarded throughout your organisation.

Organisational Standards

Some organisations lack the leadership and structure to challenge a lack of self-awareness. People who are lacking in self-awareness are moved and promoted instead of being held to account. There was a running joke in the NHS 25 years ago that people were promoted out of harm's way. They were moved up and sideways – where they didn't line manage anybody – and became some sort of senior advisor so that their behaviour could impact less people, their advice was received on a 'take it or leave it' basis and they were kept happy, quiet and well paid.

Just because an organisation's strategy says that openness and excellence are valued, doesn't mean it's actually put into practice. If the behaviours that organisational leaders promote and reward are contrary to those set out in the strategy, then what's written in the strategy will bear no resemblance to the real culture felt across the organisation.

The term 'greenwashing' became very popular in 2022 and signals organisations that say lots of eco-friendly things in their strategies but implement little to none of them. There's also 'social washing', where organisations over-exaggerate their social contributions; 'pinkwashing', where they over-egg their LGBTQIA+ support; and 'diversity washing', where they overstate their diversity, equality and inclusion activities.

There should also be a general term of 'value washing' added to the list for some organisations.

If you want to bring an organisation's strategy to life and model, encourage and celebrate the right behaviours and actions, you can do this by being clear about the organisation's standards through policies, procedures and protocols. These three types of document have an increasing level of detail on how to do things in the workplace. A policy sets out what you will do in certain circumstances, a procedure describes how you will do it and a protocol is the more detailed checklist of what exactly you need to do to discharge the procedure. Some activities won't have procedures and protocols because the policy has enough detail or because the situation has so many variables they couldn't possibly be put down in a procedure. For example, a strategy says you will not tolerate incivility and disrespect, a policy describes when you have informal management discussions and when you move to a formal disciplinary process, a procedure will tell you all the agreed templates to use to call people to disciplinary meetings and a protocol will be the checklist of things you have to say in the meeting to ensure you're tribunal-ready, should things progress to that stage.

All these documents should be aligned with the stance set out in the strategy. Common language should be used throughout these connected documents, and that language should be unambiguous and leave nothing to chance. That will mean managers and leaders are under no illusion or apprehension as to the expectations of the organisation. Of course, these things still don't guarantee that people will put them into practice. If your organisational culture is to let strategic-level leaders get away with incivility and disrespect, then that's what rules. "Culture eats strategy for breakfast," said Peter Drucker, a 20th-century management consultant who contributed to modern management theory, and he's not wrong!

As an organisational self-aware leader, it's your role to model behaviour, operate with integrity, listen to what people are telling you and live your strategy every single minute of every single day – even when no one's watching.

Recruitment

A job advert is likely to be the first contact a potential candidate has with an organisation. They may have heard about it, met someone who worked there or applied for a job there previously, but in terms of really getting to know an organisation before actually working for it, this is it. 'You don't get a second chance to make a first impression,' meaning how job adverts are written sets the tone for the organisational culture (which may or may not align with the strategy. See above!!). If self-awareness, relational skills and the nine CHARTABLE directions are important to your organisation, are they evident and obvious in job adverts? In the job description? In the questions asked at interview?

One of the self/other ratings studies said that elements of EQ associated with self-aware leadership "may provide human resource managers with selection criteria for identifying potentially effective management candidates".[1] This was back in 1999. Some organisations did, of course, embrace this and introduced the use of psychometric tests. Far less is heard about them these days, and assessing EQ and self-awareness-type characteristics, traits and behaviours is not standard practice in all recruitment processes.

I remember having an interview at Maersk Shipping in London's Canary Wharf in 1998 or '9. There were about 20 of us being interviewed for a role in their legal department. It was my first ever 'proper' interview, and I'd never heard of pre-interview assessments. There I was in my very nice navy suit, wondering why I'd been put in an exam room to answer weird questions about my preferences and behaviours. I don't recall what happened next, but I do recall the escalators in Canary Wharf and I still have the necklace I bought, so I guess it couldn't have been that traumatic. That was my first experience of psychometrics in the wild.

One of the self/other ratings studies said that self-rating of leadership ability and self-awareness were unreliable.[2] If at recruitment, all you have to go on is what the candidate tells you, there's a chance you're going to be continuing to promote the recruitment and promotion of people who can talk the talk but maybe can't walk the walk. References seem to be given less and less weight these days, and legally (in the UK anyway), previous employers have to give little more information than the answers to 'Did this person work for you?' and 'If yes, for how long?' If you're interviewing an egotistical gaslighter with just an interview made up of questions about technical skills and have nothing more than a yes/no reference to go on, there's a potential you will end up with trouble at t'mill.

I spoke to Joanna Rawbone (episode 6) about recruitment. The extraversion bias is highly evident within recruitment practices, reinforcing the idea that introverts aren't good enough, making some people feel the need to hire interview coaches to up their extraversion levels for the conversation. This is not something Joanna agrees with and leads to organisations employing people who can't sustain the facade and, ultimately, burn out when they can't maintain the pretence. Instead, it's time for introverts to own their strengths and express them confidently and for hiring managers to think more about the quality of contribution at interview, not just the quantity.

I've actually been recruiting to my team the same week as I'm writing this chapter. Only yesterday I was typing up the interview questions and I thought, *Hang on a minute, put your money where your mouth is!* I added questions like 'Tell us about the skills and behaviours you would need to do this activity?' and 'What relationship skills would you draw on to manage dissent and conflict in a situation?' In nearly 25 years in the world of work, I don't think I've ever put the word 'behaviour' into a job interview, which is quite unbelievable. Until now.

How achievable would it be for you to add 'behaviour' into a job interview question? I bet your organisational strategy sets out behaviour expectations, and I bet your management and leadership competencies mention behaviour in some guise or other. Grasp the nettle and try it out. See what happens! And see how your fellow panel members feel about it. What are you going to say to convince the dissenters?

This also raises the discussion about the organisational appreciation of cognitive diversity and neurodiversity. Recruitment is very much a one-size-fits-all approach, and anyone who's rubbish at interviews but excellent at their job is destined to coast along until someone somewhere takes a leap of faith or, as Joanna Rawbone says, fakes it at interview so they can get their foot in the door, and then works out how to transition to being themselves before they burn out.

When I spoke to Amy Gandon (episode 15), she posed the question, who are the people appointing the senior leaders of organisations? At the time, we were talking specifically about ministers in the British government and the appointment of senior civil servants, but it's a fair question to ask of all organisations. Have they come from a generation that values relational skills like empathy, compassion and self-awareness? We might need another ten years before those people are the ones who are appointing the senior people. In the meantime, what can be done to accelerate change? Can embedding self-awareness systems, such as 360-degree reviews, in a greater number of organisations bring the future closer, faster? What are your thoughts on how you can change the decisions about who gets to hold the senior jobs in your organisation, or your government?

Amy and I went on to talk about whether the modern world is skewed towards external self-awareness. If you think about Instagram and TikTok influencers, it's all about what the camera sees. Ira Wolfe (episode 24) said social media influencers were nobodies until they found their niche, and social media gave them a platform that wasn't available to them 30 years ago. If you think about politicians, are they occupationally wired to focus more on the external than the internal? Could that be why politics is cutthroat and personal, because it's all about the optics on the stage and actually all the players know the difference between when they're on the stage versus behind the curtain?

Once people are recruited, what about all the other people-management policies? Onboarding, mandatory training, supervision, performance reviews, promotions and exit interviews: there's a whole career path to consider in helping individuals on their self-aware leadership journey. Onboarding generally comes in the form of a list of documents to read, training to attend and people to meet. Mandatory training provides annual updates on the organisation's values and strategic priorities. Do all these things reinforce self-awareness, describe the expected behaviours, clarify the organisational position on hard and relational skills and emphasise the weight of importance on employee capability or conduct? Think of capability as can't cook and conduct as won't cook – one is about hard skills and the other about relational skills.

Supervision and Performance Reviews

Supervision and performance reviews are changing, and there's more chatter about ongoing reviews rather than annual reviews that happen with a flurry of activity and die like fireworks until next year's big bang. Although, it does still happen. Whether you tackle conduct and behaviour issues at these one-to-ones will be very much linked to whether you have managerial and organisational back-up to do so. Is HR available to run through a script with you? Has your manager said they'll back you with the individual and with HR? Are you emotionally prepared and have the skills and policy knowledge to take this to disciplinary if necessary?

I've worked in organisations where supervision and performance reviews haven't been separated out. Separate performance reviews went out of fashion for a while, and it was thought performance should be a discussion as and when necessary and touched on at every supervision. For the last ten years or so, I've been having weekly 30-minute one-to-ones with my direct reports where I check in on their wellbeing and generally talk about the to-do list. If there are behavioural things to pick up, I'll have either already done it as near to the 'incident' as possible or I'll pick them up here. I also like to have four-to-eight-weekly performance discussions, which are less about the what of the to-do list and more about the *how* of it.

There are different types of supervision that would be helpful to consider as a leader who's building their awareness of others' needs. In the health sector, there are structures in place for clinical and managerial supervision. The former is about supporting individuals to provide clinical care, review patient diagnoses, manage ongoing care and patient recovery and ensure effective safeguarding practices. Management supervision, on the other hand, is more about wellbeing, annual leave, sickness, time keeping, task prioritisation, etc. In social care roles, there's often a difference between caseload supervision, which may happen in groups led by a senior practitioner, and individual supervision led by the line manager.

One organisation I worked in used a template for the monthly performance review and, within it, asked the individual to describe how they had 'lived' one of the organisation's values and one of its management competencies since the last discussion. Not everybody liked the template, but I loved it! The organisation's strategy was tied with a golden thread to the performance of the individual, and the individual had to reflect on how they lived that expectation. I had many a deep and meaningful conversation with my direct reports about behaviour, managing others, psychological safety, decision making and all sorts of wonderful things using this template as a vehicle to instigate exploration. I also liked it because it was a clear acknowledgement on my part that I recognised them as being a human being, not just a human resource.

Organisational Development

Organisational development priorities in organisations are changing. The focus on hard skills is shifting more towards policy awareness and relational skills, giving people greater detail about what to do and greater autonomy in how to do it. There is still, however, a gap in individual professional development across the breadth of the layers of organisations. Professional development continues to be vested in those at the top of organisations. As Dr Gerrit Pelzer told me (episode 22), coaching is often supported and funded for those at the top of organisations because that's where strategic-level leaders think they can have the biggest impact for their investment. But if you consider that leaders can be found at all levels of organisations, coaching has the potential to support and elevate people at all levels. If you're interested in workforce retention and succession planning, this has some obvious benefits.

Many people working at the operational, business and management levels have not heard about psychological safety, the speak up agenda, the impact of incivility in the workplace and other topics of exploration in the business books and leadership thinkers community. Why aren't organisations exposing their up-and-coming staff members to this information and debate? People new to the world of work or the world of line management won't know what they don't know, so isn't it incumbent on you to expose these people and pique their interest in this stuff? If they are the future leaders and executives of your world, you need to be exposing them to and including them in thinking, debating, discussing and problem solving.

Organisations need to better support their people to understand their strengths and weaknesses and give them safe and supportive environments in which to admit their mistakes and failures. This can only be achieved when the behaviour is modelled, supported, nurtured and celebrated by strategic-level leaders. This would also help to dispel any outdated view of self-awareness as fluffy and weak and help advance better working relationships. As Dr Gerrit Pelzer said, in the corporate world, emotions are thought of as fuzzy, nebulous ideas. But your neurological impulses impact your emotions, which impact your behaviour, which impacts whether you succeed or fail in the corporate world. So maybe emotions aren't that fuzzy after all!

Wellbeing

You can't talk about workplace relationships without talking about wellbeing because this is what it's all about, isn't it? We all want to work with people on a Monday morning who don't make us feel like crap on a Sunday night. We don't want to work with colleagues and managers who prevent us from sleeping and give us a sinking feeling in the pit of our stomach, but this is absolutely the potential impact of a person with poor self-awareness.

Amy Gandon (episode 15) talked about her experience of burnout and what she'd had to learn about herself in terms of boundaries and self-care. She said, to avoid people pleasing and burnout, you must have a clear vision of 'self'. You need to know what self-care means to you before you can put it into practice. You must know what you should say no to and what you absolutely *have* to say no to. It's an observation many people miss and don't really buy into until burnout has come along and bitten them on the arse.

Organisations are still not being sufficiently explicit in their behaviour policies about the connection between self-awareness, emotional intelligence, behaviour and individual wellbeing. Wellbeing tends to be viewed more as a health, rest and relaxation thing. Organisations should, of course, be promoting their stance on wellbeing and resources for meditation, counselling, gym membership and all that sort of thing, but there's more to wellbeing than that.

Sally Evans (episode 2) said, in recent years, and more so because of Covid, power has shifted from employers to employees. This has really driven the improvements in employee engagement and wellbeing. Home working is a key factor in the power shift, as is quiet quitting and the huge gap in the labour market that's noticeable in so many different industries. (I mean, where did all the people go??)

When I spoke to Jon Rennie (episode 11), we talked about the very radical shift in organisational mindset about wellbeing that Covid foisted upon us. The workplace wellbeing perks of the noughties, like complimentary breakfast bars, free coffee and onsite gyms, were stripped away when we were all in lockdown and we experienced the wellbeing policies of organisations laid bare. Sickness policies, flexible working policies, caring policies and parental policies became the face of employee wellbeing in organisations. Where organisations didn't have these in place, or had previously relied on the superficial stuff, they had to be pretty quick in developing the policies that really mattered.

The Covid-induced wave of change has receded a little and many things are back to how they were before. Since the end of the lockdowns, some positive changes have ebbed, and some hard work needs to be done to accelerate the next flow towards improved wellbeing policies that are about the real things, not the shiny things. Sophie Bryan (episode 17) said that in her experience, some organisations are still trying to deliver on the staff wellbeing and engagement agenda with tokens and false gestures. What they're missing is the conversation about prevention being better than cure. There needs to be more talk about preventing stress, burnout, overload and poor mental health so there isn't a deviated focus back towards gimmicks and freebies.

I asked Alison Reynolds (episode 30) and Amy Zhang (episode 35), both experts in operational HR and organisational development, what they think leaders should be looking out for in the future and what employees will want from their leaders. Alison said that people's values have shifted and they are prioritising intrinsic motivation and work–life balance over monetary incentives. The pandemic highlighted the importance of family time, sabbaticals and meaningful experiences, prompting people to have open conversations about planning for a balanced and fulfilling future despite longer working lives. Amy said the traditional concept of a corporate career ladder is no longer appealing to employees. They now prioritise their own career goals and value leaders who understand and support their individual aspirations. She said younger generations have their own definitions of success and flexibility, and leaders who help them achieve their personal goals are more respected and effective. All these things take employee wellbeing and engagement in a whole different direction away from health and relaxation.

Teams

Conversations about self-awareness often lead to discussions about interactions and relationships with others and, inevitably, teams. One of the main drivers in developing self-awareness is to ensure we don't negatively impact on other people and make their work lives suck, so a thread of discussion that goes from 'me' to 'we' seems a good route to take.

In talking about teams, people often refer to 'team awareness' in the sense of getting to know how others tick, discovering others' strengths and weaknesses and engaging them in decision making. Sathpal Singh (episode 3) talked about needing to flip the narrative from 'strengths and weaknesses' to 'strengths and lesser strengths'. His view is that you should develop teams made up of people with different strengths so that, between you, you can become a team of collective strength. Neil Jurd (episode 12) said when you know your strengths, weaknesses, skills and gaps, you're in a better position to build a team around you that complements your skills and fills in the gaps. But you need to have that awareness of your gaps to work out what skills others need to bring.

Organisational leaders need to make a concerted effort to champion this awareness of strengths and proactively help others to balance their team strengths. Matt Stone (episode 10) said when a team is at risk of breaking down and there's a lack of trust and poor communication, the self-awareness of an individual is always one of the causative factors. In every workplace, there's always that one person who is a little bit more difficult and a little bit more challenging than everyone else – and every single person on the team knows who they are without having to say it. 'There's always one!', as the saying goes. Sometimes, if you're really lucky, you'll have two!

If we've ever worked together, you'll have heard me say, "20% of the people take up 80% of your time." I don't know who said it first, but I thank them for the truism. It's based on the iconic 80/20 Pareto principle, of course. When team strengths and gaps haven't been balanced out, the manager inevitably has to wade in and find a solution. I get that tackling poor or inappropriate behaviours is hard. I absolutely get it. I still think that tackling it is the right thing to do though, because without the intervention of a difficult conversation, the team imbalance is likely to capsize the boat.

Peers

Co-operation is a key element of leader effectiveness, particularly in terms of peer support. Leaders can be effective in managing their team, but in amongst a peer group of ineffective leaders, the effective leader's voice can get lost. They may find it difficult to influence and drive things forward. The literature I reviewed made little comment on interaction and co-operation between peers and between managers. I didn't specifically search it out, I admit, but it also wasn't staring me in the face either. The literature focusses mainly on vertical relationships – work life up and down the management chain of command. There wasn't much talk about horizontal relationships. I realise that's also borne out in the training I've done, and I dare say, the training you will have done too. Training sessions are generally about how to build teams and rarely talk about how to cultivate your peer group. Your line manager would have been to a training session to talk about your team, but that doesn't really help you build your peer network, does it?

Complexity leadership studies talk about interdependent agents who are "bonded together in a collective dynamic by a common need".[3] If you think back to the earlier discussion about agile teams and leadership transferring to different individuals with the right skill set depending on the project at hand, then interdependencies between people and good peer relationships are necessary elements for effective operating and will become increasingly important.

"20% of the people take up 80% of your time."

Dr Nia D. Thomas

In 2012, I did a leadership course that introduced me to much of the grown-up leadership stuff you're reading about in this book. (I'm sure you know exactly what I mean by 'grown-up'. It's the stuff of adulting. For a long time in your career, you'll have been in training sessions and meetings and felt like the discussion was not for your ears and above your pay grade. Well, this is the point of a watershed, when you realise that, actually, this stuff now sits with you. This is your job now!) One of the activities of the course was to read and review a book. I chose Patrick Lencioni's *Five Dysfunctions of a Team*. One of the earth-shattering things I took from that book was Lencioni's idea of the 'number one team'. When you ask senior leaders to tell you who their number one team is, they will usually tell you it's the group of individuals who make up their direct reports. This is the team you like to put your arms around, place a blanket on in cold weather and buy air con units for in the summer. These are your people and you are their work parent.

Wrong.

Your number one team is made up of the people to your left and to your right. We are so conditioned to look up and down that we forget we also have people on either side. When the going gets tough and you have to take your direct reports through sickness monitoring, complaints procedures, performance plans, grievances and disciplinaries, these are the people you should be able to lean on. This is, by and large, disregarded in organisations, and little is done to explicitly foster that peer support to your left and to your right. If you had to have a difficult conversation with your manager, that's where you'd want to go for sympathy, support and solutions. Think about actively putting in place networking opportunities that specifically exclude you from the conversation, in order that your direct reports can build safe, supportive peer relationships that are led or directed by you.

Communities

In the South Wales Valleys, the community is very close. People live two houses down from their mother, and their grandmother was born in the street behind. Aunties, uncles and cousins have homes at the end of the street, and friends from school and ex-partners who co-parent children reside in the next village. People know people, and that means a cross word in work spills into being a cross word in the street. Research found that community connections were seen by some as a barrier to managing staff because people didn't want to spoil relationships and upset the apple cart.

Community connections have the potential to impact on workplace atmosphere, and in my research interviews, I was told that some individuals were able to "get away with" things because of that familiarity. I mean, just remember our well-connected golfer, his influential parent and the golf club membership. It was said that, in some cases, poor behaviour was normalised because of relationships outside of work and the close connections between people. Sometimes it was challenging for managers to have difficult conversations with their direct reports about performance because, outside of work, they had some social or familial connection.

I've known of teachers who've lived in their school catchment area all their life and worked in the school for 35 years of their career. I've known of doctors who've delivered babies, babies of babies, signed death certificates of grandparents and have lived and breathed the same air as their patients. I've also been aware of community healthcare practitioners who've had to be moved to a different locality because unhappy patients knew where they lived and harassed them on their doorstep. There are three instances I can recall where there was a husband and wife working in an organisation, an affair with a third colleague, an acrimonious divorce and all the subsequent hassle of changing surnames on email accounts. I can also recall a friendship between a line manager and direct report that blossomed into a 'getting drunk together on a Saturday night at your house' and ended up going very wrong. The subordinate was eventually dismissed for, I'm sure, a 'totally unrelated issue'... hmmm.

There are benefits of familiarity – and drawbacks. I've worked in cities away from home that afforded me anonymity beyond my colleagues, teams and stakeholders. I certainly felt a different weight of expectation because of it. Although, even with that kind of anonymity, I'd occasionally bump into colleagues on the Tube or the street in a place as densely populated and busy as London.

Do any of your workplaces open the debate about whether following processes inside the organisation is going to negatively impact life for individuals outside it? Should you? If you do and they say, "Yes, if I put Leona on sickness monitoring, my husband is best friends with her father and I'll be starting a family feud," then what do you do? Your answer should be guided by your nine compass directions, and then you'll find the best path through. There will undoubtedly be some sort of trade-off, though.

Inclusive Decision Making

In the social care sector, people talk a lot about moving away from 'doing unto' to 'doing with'. There's a very strong movement away from doing things *to* service users and to doing things *with* service users. This is a major cultural shift, when for so long the mantra has been, people don't know what they need and people don't know what's good for them. There's been a stark realisation since the mid-noughties that, regardless of what people think others need, if they don't want it, they won't engage. If you think someone needs to learn to read and you put on adult literacy classes and no one comes because they want to learn to sing or play football, then maybe you need to rethink adult literacy in terms of song lyrics and football rules.

It's the same in business. If you've decided that what your clinical team needs is an extra evening cardiology clinic to get through their waiting list but you haven't asked whether anyone's available to work those hours, then what you've got is strategic-level disconnect. And what you need is inclusive decision making.

A major roadblock to effective self-aware leadership, which you'll read more about in the next chapter, is strategic-level disconnect. It's that lack of connection between the people at the strategic level of the organisation making the decisions and those people at the operational end who are tasked with implementing them. An enabler for this is inclusive decision making. Inclusive decision making bridges the gap of detachment between the strategic and operational functions within organisations.

There is a link between detachment, emotions and decision making because feelings are linked to the way people make decisions, think and behave.[4] Relations-orientated leadership involves behaviour that explicitly includes subordinates in decision making.[5] In the discussion about resilience and wellbeing leadership, inclusive decision making is referenced in the definition. Including people in decision making is a mitigator against strategic-level disconnect, and it impacts people's emotional attachment, feelings of purpose, contribution, acknowledgement and, ultimately, happiness in the workplace.

Alison Lagier (episode 7) said that because feedback is filtered at the strategic level, people operating at that level need to actively seek out input from others. Without that input, it might mean they can't achieve their goal, and their plans end up being simply underivable. Alison's advice? Take people with you on your journey. A project might be longer in the planning, but delivery is going to be more attainable. Because you've put the effort up front in the planning, the delivery part of the process will be shorter, smoother and more likely to end up with a positive outcome. If you don't, the planning may be far shorter, but the delivery's going to be fraught with problems and obstacles and you'll have lots of unhappy people challenging you when you think you're near the finishing line. Front load your time and weight your engagement to planning rather than rectification. Your pocket will probably be better off too.

Organisations need to consider innovative methods to ensure inclusive decision making isn't tokenistic and is really valued. You need to think more about co-production as the way you do things, which is a level of commitment and resource allocation significantly greater than the predominantly consultative way organisations usually involve people in decision making. Organisations are forever distributing surveys that ask questions like "We're going to be closing down our second office.

Are you okay with that?" and feeding back that there weren't enough responses to make the 'nopes' statistically significant and, therefore, they're ploughing ahead as proposed. They then have to deal with those unhappy people waving placards two feet from the finish line.

Liam Maguire (episode 19) said the best leaders push authority and information down through organisations to allow other people to make decisions. Organisations that retain decision making at the top are missing opportunities to innovate and make the best decisions for the customer, patient or service user. Mission command, the military approach to decision making, empowers people at all levels to make the right decision in the right place at the right time. This resonates with our earlier exploration into organisations that continue to operate in the 'pyramid shape' of the industrial paradigm versus those that are moving to a more fluid and adaptable structure in response to changing demands of knowledge-based work.

In the Rear-View Mirror

You've trekked down the beautiful slopes of strategy and sojourned the soaring mountains of supervision. You've climbed the cliffs of communities and traversed the rapids of teams. You've explored the highway code of self-aware leadership for those helpful signposts and directions that enable you to steam ahead on your superhighway, knowing your route is well-lit, clearly planned and your fellow travellers know all about being courteous to other superhighway users.

A conscientious self-aware leader focussed on improving their behaviour in the nine CHARTABLE directions can't, of course, do it alone. Self-aware leadership, as a socially constructed concept, is reliant on relationships. When you add other people onto your superhighway – people with their own ideas, thoughts, abilities and biases – without signposts and directions, you're going to end up clashing and crashing. If you want to prevent your organisation from being a train wreck, be relationship-focussed, be people-focussed and use signposts and directions to guide you around those roadblocks and trip hazards, which I'm going to tell you about next.

Huddle up as your journey along the superhighway takes you into the dark side, where the Venus fly traps are as big as your head and the snow-covered chasms hide a never-ending abyss of misery.

Come on! Hold tight!

7. ROADBLOCKS AND TRIP HAZARDS

Chapter Map

Where there is light, there is always a balancing dark. What goes up must come down. Every yin has a yang. When travelling on your journey of self-aware leadership, there are things to enable you and things to disable you. In the previous chapter, you explored signposts and directions that guided your journey, and now we turn to the roadblocks and trip hazards that will obstruct you.

You'll take a ride through strategic-level disconnect and the impact of detachment, and be prepared to get tied up in the red tape of bureaucracy. Then you'll take a helicopter flight above the smoking embers of crises and stress and put on your gas mask as you descend into psychological toxicity. You'll leave the dark valley via the spaghetti junction of accidental leaders and hope that you emerge on the other side with your faculties intact and your mind recovered.

Helmets on, Kevlar suits zipped up, night vision goggle straps securely tightened. Stealth mode engaged. Let's do this!

Disconnection and Detachment

Strategic-level disconnect was a big issue that appeared in my research – with neon lights. Research interviewees said there was a disconnect between strategic-level decision making and operational-level implementation. Strategic ideas were flawed by the time they reached the point of implementation. Strategic-level managers had little awareness of the impact of their decisions, and messages from the top were distorted by the time they reached the shop floor. This was felt to be the case both within organisations as well as between them. When one organisation was commissioning another to deliver a service, there was a disconnect between the contractual asks and the operational ability to deliver. This is an interesting comment and connects us to the challenges of system-wide working and our earlier discussion about systems thinking.

Strategic-level disconnect was also linked to care, with one person telling me:

**"It appears that the higher you get at management level,
the less you care about others and just look out for yourself."**

Ouch. This is a damning indictment of leader behaviour.

One organisation appeared to have established its promotion culture on the ability of individuals to implement difficult strategic decisions rather than their ability to demonstrate good people-leadership, to the point that the interviewee felt this could be due to an inability to spot social cues and grasp others' emotions. They told me this was a more palatable viewpoint to hold because the alternative was to deduce that they just didn't care.

Beyond the structures and systemic roadblocks that lead to strategic-level disconnect, you do need to consider individual detachment. We talk about organisations as if they are organic entities or sentient beings, but of course, they're not. They're just groups of people like you, that do particular things, have particular beliefs and behave in particular ways. That's why detachment as a thing related to individual leaders is relevant to you in your quest for self-awareness and effective self-aware leadership.

Detachment is a contributary behaviour of leader derailment.[1] Leaders who operate in dissonance with other people impact on the effectiveness of individuals and organisations as a whole.[2] That's relevant to you because if resonant leadership is based on emotional intelligence, then dissonant leadership is a lack of emotional intelligence, and emotional intelligence is used interchangeably with self-awareness. Resilience and wellbeing are impacted when leaders feel overwhelmed. When "leaders are disengaged" and "shut themselves away", they operate in the zone of their "worst selves".[3]

Gunther Verheyen (episode 5) told me he'd worked in a company that was part of the dot.com boom in the late 1990s. He was still working there when the bubble burst. He'd been part of the senior team responsible for identifying people to fire. He'd really struggled with it but found it even more difficult to deal with his CEO, who seemed to be emotionless throughout the process. Gunther pinned his boss down for a heart-to-heart conversation about his lack of emotion. The CEO said he kept his emotions for after work and for his wife and family. Gunther said that was a turning point for him – he didn't want to end up like that, devoid of emotion in his work and towards his colleagues. If that isn't an example of emotional detachment, I don't know what is.

Gunther said it's inhumane to expect people to hide their emotions in the workplace. When people climb the career ladder, it's as if they leave their human side behind. But this isn't normal, it's not natural and, in the long term, it's just not sustainable. It adds to individuals' stress and overlays pressure on people to behave inauthentically, eventually exacerbating the work pressures that lead to burnout. Similarly, Jeroen Kraaijenbrink (episode 16) said some strategic leaders appear not to be self-reflective or have lost their ability to be self-reflective. It's difficult to pin down whether this means they're not self-aware or whether they're putting on a mask so as not to show their vulnerability. When a leader gets anxious or worried, it permeates through an organisation, and maybe some leaders are conflating vulnerability with inability. The bigger the company, the greater the pressure to be that strong leader that others want you to be.

Strategic-level disconnect is something that proliferates right through companies, but it doesn't have to. Just because the culture of your organisation acquiesces to this kind of them-and-us-ness, it doesn't mean that you, as the journeying self-aware leader, have to follow suit. If all of the other five executives in your company like the anonymity of the office with the closed door, it doesn't mean you have to do the same. You can introduce co-production, engagement and feedback opportunities within your team. When you explore feedback in Part 3, it'll give you ideas about how to remove this roadblock.

Red Tape

Red tape and bureaucracy are potential barriers to effective leadership, notably leadership at all levels, because of the policy and procedural restrictions ubiquitous within bureaucratic organisations.[4] This was particularly relevant to my research because I was investigating the public sector, and public-sector organisations are generally viewed as bureaucratic.

Bureaucratic organisations tend to be very process-bound, making them inflexible and slow, with decisions being made at clearly defined points – usually somewhere near the top, increasing the potential for exclusive decision making. The public and charitable sectors are preoccupied with corporate governance for the very simple reason they're using other people's money. If you work in a big commercial organisation, you've probably experienced something similar and the whole organisation bristles with nervous energy when the board is about to convene.

Corporate governance is the governing and decision-making structure of an organisation. The elements that often make up that governance structure are the board of directors and its sub-groups; their terms of reference, detailing who they are accountable to and what they are responsible for; the timing of those groups – usually linked to financial reporting deadlines, membership and representation; the declarations of interest of those members; the reports that are presented; the risk logs that are updated and shared; and the minutes and action logs that are taken and ratified. All these things were developed to enhance accountability, transparency, auditability and inclusivity, but it's undeniably made organisations cumbersome, slow and inflexible and the whole process needs a lot of resources to co-ordinate and manage it.

In my first and second jobs, I worked as an administrator in the corporate teams of two large NHS trusts, meaning I was initiated into corporate governance early on in my career. I remember seeing packs and packs of trust board papers being printed and bound, each about three-quarters of an inch thick. The white papers at the front were for public consumption, the green papers were for private board discussions and the pink papers at the back were for a sub-set of the private board, which generally happened before the public board. The organisation, collation and production of those packs was a stressful time, and no one dared interrupt the secretary to the board when they were in flow. One misjudged interruption and a paper might be rubber-stamped with the wrong enclosure number, meaning a reprint and depletion of the special-coloured paper stock. Each complete pack was finally put in a brown envelope, piled high for the postal collection and delivered a week before the board meeting. The move to digital papers and iPads wasn't a change to everyone's liking, but for people servicing those big decision-making meetings, they were a godsend.

In my second job, I was involved in things like managing the organisation's declarations of interest register, reviewing organisational compliance with the standing orders and standing financial instructions and reporting to the audit committee. Both roles taught me a huge deal about the internal workings of organisations (as well as organisational politics) and, as a newbie to the world of work, gave me valuable insight into the workings of highly bureaucratic organisations, which are still relevant to most organisations twenty-blah years later.

There was a discernible flex in corporate governance during Covid, when an alternative structure was stood up in the health service. The usual trust board and sub-group structure was paused in lieu of bronze, silver and gold command, which met more frequently, recorded actions more briefly, challenged outcome delivery more ruthlessly and generally operated more like governance in a war zone, which I guess it was in the very early days. Emergency governance procedures will have been planned and agreed far in advance of the pandemic, but the speed at which the procedures were stood up and mobilised was both impressive and frightening, demonstrating that individuals, teams and organisations can be flexible, responsive and adaptable when they need to be.

But, of course, there is evidence that individuals are learning to lead, regardless of the constraints of red tape, through an adaptive leadership model.[5] In *The Attributes*, Rich Diviney talks about trying to draw the operational leadership model of a US Navy SEAL team on a whiteboard. He writes:

> **"The most obvious was the classic pyramid with a leader at the top and widening layers of subordination below... The military, with its hierarchical chain of command, is basically a giant pyramid. But that didn't seem to fit a SEAL team... I briefly considered the flat model... I stood there for a few moments, pondering my options. Finally, and mostly in frustration, I drew what looked like an amoeba. A blob...**
> **In a high-performance team, leadership shifts to wherever, and whomever, the leader needs to be at any given moment. Those teams understand that information, challenges, and obstacles can come from any angle at any time. And they're effective because the team mate closest to the problem is able to step up and lead, while the rest of the group defers to that temporary leader... I call this, my amoeba-shaped organizational plan, dynamic subordination."**

Dynamic subordination allows SEAL teams to operate a complexity leadership model within a bureaucratic organisation, which might be the way traditional industrial paradigm-type organisations will be able to capitalise on different forms of leadership and different demands from employees as we journey through the third decade of the 21st century.

Crises and Stress

'Non-routine events', 'black swan events', 'wicked problems'[6] and 'VUCA' (volatile, unexpected, complex and ambiguous) – the unfamiliar and unexpected 'new crises' situations have many names. Whatever you call them, organisations are facing a growing number of increasingly complex situations. They have experienced the biggest crisis the world has seen since the Spanish flu in 1918 and the Black Death in the 14th century.

Covid was the crisis of all crises (so far!). On top of that, people are dealing with the lingering aftermath of the financial crash of 2008; the cost of living crisis that burgeoned in 2022 caused by Covid, Brexit, the war in Ukraine and greed, and lots of other things that politicians want to blame it on; the floods and wildfires caused by the climate crisis; and to top it off there's artificial intelligence and the impending doom that is being predicted by its founding forefathers. It's a lot.

No single person, department or organisation has the sole means to deal with problems like these, and working across traditional boundaries is essential.[7] This style of working is called 'unity of effort' and has five dimensions of leadership. The first being 'understanding oneself and one's emotions', which is to all intents and purposes internal self-awareness. Then there's understanding the event or the challenge, leading upwards between political leaders and experts, leading downwards to support the people and leading across organisational boundaries. The last three are all about relationship management and, thus, recognition and regulation feature significantly. A 2013 article says leadership beyond boundaries and beyond spans of authority would become more important in the future,[8] and it wasn't wrong. Pandemic aside, in the UK, there's definitely greater direction from government for public- and charitable-sector organisations to work closer together and move to a place where systems thinking and systems working is how you get things done.

Distributed leadership is seen as best practice in managing in a crisis; where there's "a complex adaptive challenge... a top-down hierarchical approach is unlikely to be successful... Distributing leadership responsibilities is more effective than other leadership approaches in a crisis."[9] That's also what Diviney said of what successful leadership looked like in SEAL teams. One piece of advice that Neil Jurd (episode 12) gave from his Army career was, train so that what you need, whether that's a skill or a process or a way of bringing yourself to a place of calm, is ready for you to call on in a crisis.

One thing the Army is very good at, he said, is training its people, reflecting on what happened, refining and training again. If you train your people and equip them with effective and useful skills, when they're in a crisis situation, they can dip into their toolbox and draw on their learning to get them through without having to worry about where the manual or instruction video is. They'll be so familiar with the process that it's at the forefront of their mind, tip of their tongue and ends of their fingers. Train hard, fight easy!

For a period of about three years, I ran. When I started, I got a running coach to help me get the basics right. He said, "Breathe in for three and out for two." "Always do this when you run", he said, "because it'll become second nature. Breathe this way when you're running steady so that when your energy is depleting, it's there for you when you need it." It's the same idea: practise something enough so that it becomes ingrained, meaning you can call on it when you're under stress and in a crisis.

When someone is in crisis or feeling threatened, it will be their emotions that drive behaviour.[10] You know that a leader's self-awareness is dynamic rather than static, and you know that it fluctuates in response to stimuli like stress.[11] L. David Marquet writes that pressures, deadlines and stressors have a positive or neutral effect on redwork (doing), but they deplete the same cognitive resource that is needed for bluework (thinking). If, then, feelings are linked to the way people think, behave and make decisions[12] in times of stress, people might miss signs from others that give them cues about how to manage themselves and their relationships and interactions in a particular situation.[13]

Tracy Myhill (episode 18) said that workload and the behaviours of others impact on your stress levels. Stress, in turn, impacts and influences your behaviour, meaning you show up at your worst. The more stressed you are, the worse you behave. She also told me how important it was to have trusted colleagues around you in these situations to recognise your downward spiral (or building explosion) and who can tell you, respectfully, that you need to go for a walk or grab a bite to eat.

Stress responses have implications on your ability to be self-aware in the moment. A stressed leader who once may have been able to relate to their people is now operating on autopilot, driven by their sympathetic nervous system on overdrive. They're rubbing colleagues up the wrong way, snapping, raising their voices or, conversely, paralysed and unable to make decisions. This quickly impacts on their close colleagues and eventually ripples out to the rest of the organisation.[14] When leaders are in these kinds of situations, where there's increased work pressure, they might behave out of character, exhibiting physical and mental disruption, and they may become emotionally detached from the organisation.[15]

There are five stated principles for leadership during a crisis: stay calm, communicate, collaborate, co-ordinate and support.[16] To act with deliberate calm,[17] a leader needs to know themselves well enough to know how they respond to stress and how they're likely to deal with it in a crisis. They need to be able to "communicate clearly and frequently"[18] so that they can facilitate and co-ordinate the collaboration that's needed between colleagues and still have sufficient empathy to support people through their own anxieties to get the job done. All five of these principles need an underpinning of self-awareness. In her October 2020 TED Talk, 'How to lead in a crisis', Amy Edmondson said the usual tropes of leadership – namely strength, confidence and constancy – don't work in a crisis. You need to be transparent, act with urgency, follow your values and share power. Check it out. At my last count, it had been watched over 790,000 times.

Lots of people ask, "Can too much self-awareness be a bad thing?" Self-awareness is undoubtedly a good thing, but if reflection becomes rumination, taking you into a spiral of overthinking and poor mental health, then it's not a good thing. When you're under stress, you need to keep the cycle of reflection, recognition and regulation in motion and move on rather than linger and dwell on the reflection or recognition stage. If stress causes you to get stuck, that isn't healthy or helpful, and getting out of stuck-ness due to overthinking is hard mental work.

"In a crisis, perhaps the most important [practice] of all is emotional intelligence and emotional stability that will allow the... leader to place the interests of others above their own..."[19] When you're dealing with your own physiological and mental distress, reaching down deep to find your emotional intelligence is not easy. Sally Evans (episode 2) said that when leaders are lacking in reflection and thinking time, and suffering from both stress and exhaustion, they form barriers to effective self-awareness and effective leadership. Even if your general leadership practice is to reflect and be reflective, you're going to be prevented from doing so because of stress, exhaustion and a lack of time. There's a clear trajectory: as crises and stress build, self-awareness and emotional intelligence diminish for the simple reason that the body moves its focus from higher awareness to just surviving. When stress has your blood pressure skyrocketing and your heart pounding, it really is about just keeping your body functioning in that moment.

Psychological Toxicity

For a long time, I've been trying to find an opposite term to 'psychological safety'. The web gave me 'psychological danger' and 'psychological threat', but I'm wondering if 'psychological toxicity' fits better? Danger feels like something connected to tigers and stepladders. Threat feels like something connected to machetes and cyber hackers. Toxicity feels more like an oozing swamp of sticky green chemicals that are slowly burning your feet and fingers off whilst corroding your soul from the inside. It aptly fits the feeling you get when you're in an un-psychologically safe work situation, don't you think?

In *The Fearless Organizations*, the book by the renowned founder of psychological safety, Amy Edmondson, psychological safety is defined as "a belief that one will not be punished or humiliated for speaking up with ideas, questions, concerns or mistakes and that the team is safe for interpersonal risk-taking". Psychological toxicity is the opposite. An infographic by offbeat-yoga.com lists signs of a toxic workplace as poor communication, unsupportive leadership, negative outlooks and no work–life balance.

I once worked on the 'Speak Up' programme team at an NHS trust. The programme, based on the 2011 Vanderbilt model, was intended to increase psychological safety in the organisation, both for the clinical teams and the corporate teams. When colleagues want to speak up but don't feel able to do so directly to the individual, they can go via a third party, called the peer messenger. They give non-judgemental feedback to the individual by conveying the message without divulging names or breaking confidences. It's an incredibly powerful model and takes the sting out of difficult conversations whilst ensuring difficult conversations are still had.

In a 2021 webinar, Prof. Duncan Lewis shared some statistics evidencing the impact workplace incivility and disrespect in the NHS has on individuals, their colleagues and, ultimately, patients. The data was pretty damning. The NHS's Civility and Respect Toolkit was being launched, and it was inspiring. In a July 2021 webinar by the Cognitive Institute, focussing on civility in the workplace, a wealth of academic research was presented that evidenced the negative and frequently dangerous impact that even low-level incivility has on people. Incivility impairs your cognitive functioning, meaning you operate below the standards your role requires. This is true whether that incivility is directed at you or whether you are a bystander.

The work by Dr Chris Turner at Civility Saves Lives is fascinating. Look his TED Talk up and listen to the conversation he had on *The Power of Murmuration* podcast, episode five, which is simply inspirational. He's a straight talker and he'll give you the message, clear and concise, no frills and no blather. If you're interested in psychological safety and anti-bullying in the workplace, you definitely need to check out the NHS Toolkit, the Vanderbilt Promoting Professionalism model and Dr Turner at Civility Saves Lives.

I've talked to several podcast guests about what generates psychologically toxic workplaces, and we've explored things like prioritising key performance indicators over people, narcissistic players who make immoral choices, having to work around ineffective leaders and get on despite them, and organisations whose culture is so poor it pays to have low emotional intelligence to work there!!

Sophie Bryan (episode 17) talked about strategic-level leadership and agreed that it's often more about the results than the relationships. In commercial organisations, it's primarily a numbers game: a financial profits game. If the KPIs are being achieved and the money is rolling in, does it matter, and do we care? We got on to talking about employee engagement and organisational prioritisation of employees. If you think about retail, it's an area of high staff turnover. This is often because customers and results are prioritised over staff and relationships, which reflects the discussion between Stephen Shedletzky and Tiffani Bova I referenced in the section about the compass point of care in Chapter 5. If you want to move organisations to being places where people feel valued, respected and want to work, boards need to prioritise employee happiness over customer satisfaction. Remember what Richard Branson said? Look how it's worked out for him!!

Síle Walsh (episode 14), who has a research interest in inclusive leadership in for-profit organisations, also explored this in our discussion. Leading for results isn't the same as leading for the people. When organisations reward leaders who don't support others to thrive, it perpetuates the appointment of people with low relational skills into leadership positions. Some leaders know how to play the game well simply because they know the rules, not because they support others to thrive.

When you talk about leaders who are more interested in the numbers than the people, you find yourself going down the alley of discussing people with limited self-awareness. When I talked to Robertson Hunter Stewart (episode 8), he told me about the experiences he'd had in the hotel industry, managing big hotels and large hotel companies. When there are ineffective executive leaders in an organisation, the senior management team has to take the weight of responsibility for leading the organisation and delivering on objectives. The quantum of weight the senior leadership team has to hold depends on the severity of the ineffectiveness at the executive level. When the burden of holding the weight falls on the shoulders of those outside the senior team and the structural layer below, the future of the organisation is very much under threat. Once you open Pandora's office door, it's almost impossible to get all the secrets back in.

Matthew Phelan (episode 13) shared an interesting perspective about self-awareness and sensitivity. He suggested self-awareness can be a good thing and a bad thing. If you're in a flourishing culture, being self-aware can help you relate to others. You draw on your empathy and sensitivity to help you operate effectively. But if you're in an organisation with a toxic culture, the less empathic and sensitive you are, the less you'll worry about other people's opinions and carry on regardless! That's a sad state of affairs, but nevertheless, absolutely true. Matthew gives politics as an example of where this plays out...

Accidental Leaders

I once sat on the interview panel for a finance team leader role. The candidate demonstrated a high level of technical proficiency in financial recording and reporting but throughout the interview they were unable to make eye contact with the panel, use language that was non-technical and they couldn't reassure us in any way that they would be able to build an effective team. If they had been appointed, it would have been a disaster for them and the team. They would have lost confidence, respect and probably not made it through the probationary period. However, their level of technical expertise was such that I found myself, a week or two later, emailing their manager to share a job advert for a senior technical expert role with them in the hope that the person would apply. They would have been perfect.

One of the fundamental barriers to self-aware leadership that impacts an individual and radiates out to a team is 'accidental leadership'. When people with expertise in particular hard skills find themselves being promoted into people management roles, regardless of whether they have the relational skills to do the job, this is accidental leadership. In my research, my interviewees said things like "A manager will be appointed as they're technically competent at their role, but they will not necessarily have the leadership qualities required to bring their team along with them" and "Intelligence and other behavioural things don't necessarily come hand in hand." There really is a need for relational skills, not just hard skills, when jobs entail people management functions.

Leadership and people management are often conflated, but they aren't the same thing. Carly Cannings (episode 27), founder of The Happy Business School, said the traditional path to leadership involved excelling in a technical role, and then someone would decide that you'd reached your peak and... "Here! We'll give you some people to manage!" Jon Rennie (episode 11) said some people are considered effective 'individual contributors', and because of their skill, they're moved into management positions, often without the right support and training. That leads to a misunderstanding of the leadership functions embedded in management and an inability to engage with teams, leading to challenges in retaining the workforce.

Sophie Bryan (episode 17) talked about her husband, who *was* the technical expert. He experienced, first hand, this situation playing out. He was a technical expert and was promoted into a people management position. He found himself unhappy, unfulfilled and not playing to his strengths. He eventually left the organisation because he decided the promotion just wasn't for him. Sophie said you need to separate out the two skill sets and allow people to play to their strengths. To do this, people need to be self-aware about their strengths, weaknesses, values and purpose to help them make decisions about finding a better fit in a different role.

In the Rear-View Mirror

You've taken a ride on the dark side and come out into the light, but I can't guarantee there won't be any residual trauma. You may have spent time in organisations where strategic-level disconnect or bullying was so prevalent that it left you fighting for your wellbeing and battling burnout. These roadblocks and trip hazards may be all too familiar to you, and you can tell your own stories about the negative impacts and radiating influence of the dark shadows cast by leaders who are not working to create psychologically safe workplaces.

You've journeyed through the depths of disconnection and detachment and explored the impact on being able to deliver operational goals. You've rowed through the rapids of red tape and felt the ropes of bureaucracy tighten around you to the point where you feared you'd drown. You've pressed the hazard warning lights to let other superhighway users know that you're in a crisis and under stress. You've waded through the swamp of psychological toxicity and felt it seep into your boots, down your collar and into your soul. You've finally reached the end of the dark side and can see a flicker of light beyond the valley of accidental leaders.

You're glad to be beyond the dark side but recognise that many others travel to work there every day. As a self-aware leader, you need to reduce the size of the dark lands by shining a light at their edges to make them recede and wither.

Put the headlights of the bullet car on full beam, Parker!

You need to train and prepare your staff, employees and colleagues to be ready to respond to wicked events when lianas of red tape wind around their necks and the toxic ooze threatens to engulf them. You need to prepare yourself too. You have to be ready to lead, to hand power over to others, to facilitate, direct, co-ordinate and respond, drawing on the knowledge and skills you've built up from having journeyed in all nine directions of the self-awareness compass and learnt something along the way.

Let's head into the transfer lounge of Part 2 to reflect on your journey through 'Where' before you head into Part 3, your journey of 'How'.

THE TRANSFER LOUNGE: PART 2

As you come to the end of Part 2 of your guidebook, you now have a chance to grab a shower in the VIP lounge and wash off the toxic slime. Then you can have a sit down and reflect on your journey of nine directions, the valley of light and the dale of darkness.

On to the model of self-aware leadership that you explored in Transfer Lounge 1; we can now overlay the nine compass points, signposts and directions, and roadblocks and trip hazards to create the expanded self-aware leadership compass chart:

You need to travel along the routes of care, humility, authenticity, reflection, trust, adaptability, behaviour, listening and experience as far as you can, aiming for mastery in all nine directions. You need to create robust signposts and directions in your organisation, focussing on strategy, planning, and people-related policies and practices. You need to consider team functioning and the role of peers and communities in enabling you and others to function to the best of your abilities and develop into the best self-aware leader you can be. You also need to facilitate inclusive decision making to give your organisation the best chance of success possible.

You need to be aware of and minimise the negative impacts of the roadblocks and trip hazards that have developed in the industrial paradigm that might no longer be helpful to you as you zoom into the knowledge-based paradigm. You need to be aware of disconnect and detachment and build a bridge to engage people earlier and more

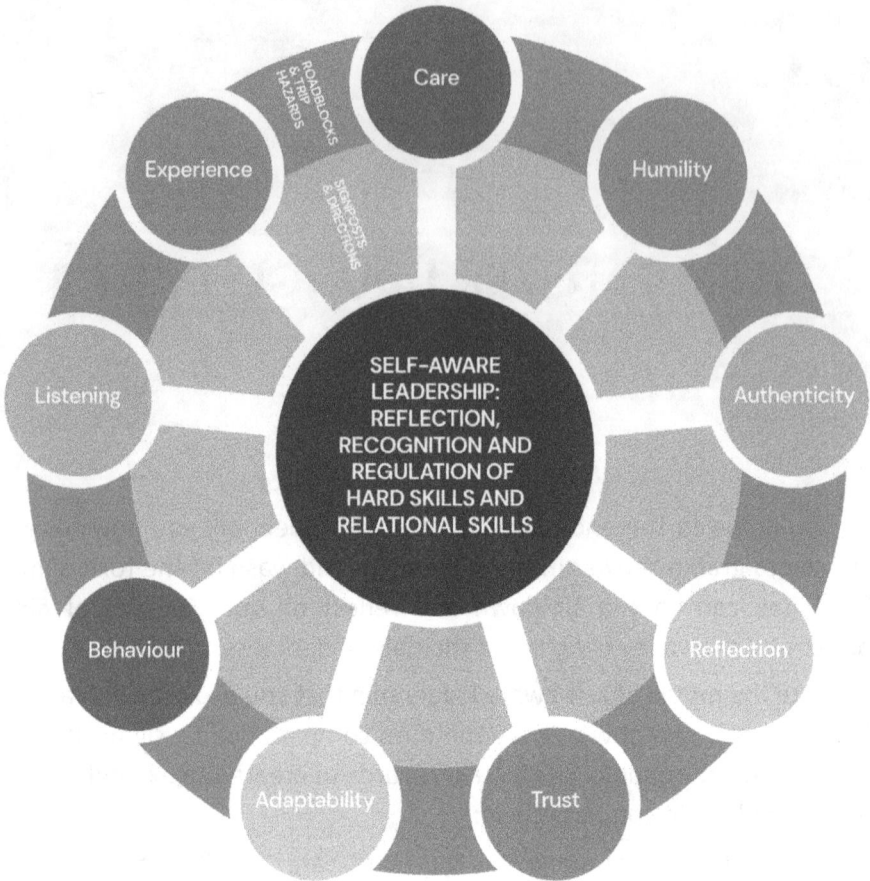

fundamentally. You need to sever the red tape that binds you, that makes you slow and unresponsive. You need to prepare, plan and train for crises whilst minimising the dangerous impacts of stress. You need to reduce psychological toxicity and cultivate psychological safety through building knowledge of yourself and others. You also need to ensure you don't accidentally place people in leadership positions that tarnish their brightness and prevent them from allowing their strengths to shine.

Your journey along the superhighway was never going to be plain sailing. The more time you spend on the highway, the more likely you are to come up against potholes, roadworks, accidents and broken-down vehicles. The more time you spend as a leader on your unique Self-Awareness Superhighway, the more you will learn and grow in hard skills and relational skills. To do that, you must experience both the light and dark side of leadership. When you learn from the tough stuff, you also grow into the good stuff, making you better prepared for the next thousand miles of your journey along your superhighway.

Enough looking back in that rear-view mirror. You have a superhighway to travel and more to explore. Let's head off into the sunset to see what tomorrow brings.

PART 3
HOW WILL YOU GET THERE?

8. TRAVEL GUIDES

Chapter Map

This guidebook has taken you along the superhighway from 'Why' in Part 1 to 'Where' in Part 2, and now you've reached 'How' in Part 3.

In 'Part 1 – Why are you here, traveller?', you explored what this book is all about and read the definitions and descriptions of self-awareness, leader effectiveness and leadership at all levels. You explored why self-aware leadership is important to you in your day-to-day work and how knowing the self allows you to know others better. And in knowing others better, it helps you to know yourself better still.

In 'Part 2 – Where are you going?', you explored the nine CHARTABLE compass directions of care, humility, authenticity, reflection, trust, adaptability, behaviour, listening and experience. You also travelled through the organisational and collegiate signposts and directions that enable you, and you sojourned between and around the roadblocks and trip hazards that disable you.

Now you're here in 'Part 3 – How will you get there?' Here, you'll explore tools and techniques that will help you voyage onward, empowered and informed on your journey of self-aware leadership. You'll explore mindfulness and meditation; tests, tools and assessments; journaling; coaching, mentoring and supervision; feedback; 360-degree reviews; and your very own Compass Quiz, designed especially for you as part of this guide.

All aboard the omnibus! Please have your tickets ready to show the conductor!

Mindfulness and Meditation

In 2004, I became sick with no clinically discernible cause. For about five months, I moved home to my parents' and slowly improved by sleeping a lot, setting myself some daily challenges and exploring acupuncture, reflexology, cranial osteopathy, homeopathy and other forms of complementary healing. When I got better and went back to work, my friend stumbled upon a reflexology course I could attend at weekends whilst still working full time. In 2006, I qualified as a reflexologist. I became interested in meditation at the same time. I often used it as part of my reflexology practice, particularly when clients came to me for a session and spent the first 20 minutes talking at me like a machine gun. I'd take them through a few breathing exercises or a guided meditation to calm their mind so the reflexology could mend their body. I practised until 2016, when I went back to uni to do my doctorate, but still use it with family and achy colleagues today, with a view to it being my retirement career one day.

One of the most fundamental tools for developing self-awareness is mindfulness and mindful meditation. These are tools that are always available to you. You don't need a fancy mat or expensive trainers; all you need is to decide you want to do it (and to not be in traffic, obviously). Mindfulness helps you engage with the very core of your being – your breath, your heartbeat and your thoughts. If you think of Maslow's hierarchy of needs, physiological needs are at the very foundation, with the layers of safety and security, love and belonging, and self-esteem building one on top of the other, right up to the layer of self-actualisation at the apex of the iconic pyramid. Mindfulness helps you tap into that physiological bedrock to understand what your body needs on that very basic level. It takes you from being in your head to being in your body.

Mindfulness isn't new but it's had a very evident resurgence in the last decade or so. Jon Kabat-Zinn is the founder of what we think of as today's work-based mindfulness. He developed it in 1979 and called it mindfulness-based stress reduction (MBSR). You can access Kabat-Zinn's meditations via his app: JKZ Meditations. There's a great introduction section, 'Mindfulness for Beginners', which you might want to explore.

I spoke to author, life coach and committed free spirit Anna Zannides (episode 45), who raised some concerns about our societal preoccupation with shiny things and how the breadth of mindfulness has been distilled to the 'shiny' element of relaxation. She said that, really, the power of mindfulness is in the introspection and self-inquiry it fosters. It's about understanding your internal world, your internal environment and what's going on inside you.

One organisation I worked in started running six-week mindfulness courses, and to put it into practice, I occasionally started my team meeting with five minutes of guided meditation. The first workplace course I actually attended was many years later. We followed Williams and Penman's *Mindfulness: A Practical guide to Finding Peace in a Frantic World*, which is an eight-week course of guided meditation that you can find on SoundCloud. During Covid, I attended a virtual group where one person led about 300 people in a guided meditation. A number of organisations are now paying for subscriptions to apps like Headspace and Calm.

I spoke to Andrew Sewell (episode 37), a coach, recovering overthinker and a former creative and copywriter who coaches leaders to overcome their overthinking. In his book, *The Overthinker's Guide to Life*, he offers 28 exercises to reduce overthinking. Andrew shares valuable insights about his journey of recovery from overthinking, emphasising the importance of changing your relationship with your thoughts. Andrew said self-awareness goes beyond surface-level knowledge: it requires exploration of your unconscious thoughts, ingrained behaviours and learning patterns.

Reiner Kraft (episode 43) is the founder of The Mindful Leader and one of Silicon Valley's most prolific inventors. He focusses his attention on mindfulness for tech leaders. He experienced stress and burnout and learnt about mindfulness for his own benefit, which he now shares with others. Reiner told me about 'mindful minutes' and 'level of present awareness' (LPA). He said, start with doing ordinary things mindfully, like brushing your teeth, taking a shower, walking the dog, etc. Be fully present; focus on the experience – what's happening inside of you, outside of you and around you – with all of your senses.

This is how you create mindful minutes. These mindful minutes accumulate: brushing your teeth mindfully gives you two minutes, having a shower mindfully gives you 20 minutes, eating a strawberry mindfully, one minute, and so on. To calculate your LPA, you take the average number of hours you're awake and make them into minutes. For an average person on an average day, that gives you about 1,000 minutes. Add up your mindful minutes: 2 + 20 + 1 = 23. That gives you an LPA of 2.3%. The goal is between 10 and 20% of LPA per day. Taking a more scientific approach and using hard numbers attracts people with a more scientific bent who might otherwise find the concept of mindfulness a bit woo woo. This feels very achievable. You don't have to drive to the gym and stay there for 45 minutes; you just have to brush your teeth. Oh wait, you do that already??

On the JKZ Meditations app, there's a 'silence with bells' facility. It's basically a timer to allow you to do some personal meditation with a bell at the end to notify you your time's up. You can set it for up to 4 hours and 49 minutes. You can also set up interval bells to chime at 4-, 5-, 10-, 15- and 20-minute intervals. This is such a great tool for building mindful minutes. A pet peeve of both mine and my husband is meditations that go silent and then people's voices come back in and frighten the bejesus out of you. Not great for sleep-time meditations! Combine this timer with some Tibetan bells via your favourite music streaming service and you're onto a winning combination.

When I was commuting on the London Underground, I'd use two techniques. Tube trains are very loud and screechy, so I started listening to the noises beyond those of the train. It was surprising the voices, music, squeaky pieces of luggage and dropped mobile phones you could hear! It was a good way to use the journey practically and helped me redirect my focus away from my monkey mind. Sometimes I would focus on the sensation and movement of the train under my feet. If you like quiet places, the Tube can be overwhelming, so this is a good way to move your attention from your head to your feet. My idea was that if I practised meditation when I didn't need it, it would be a better honed skill for when I did – a bit like the 3:2 breathing advice for runners.

I once joined a walking meditation group between one or other of the Covid lockdowns, in a London park. Throughout the walk, the leader guided us to focus on some very specific things related to our senses: what can you hear in the furthest reaches of your hearing? How many colours of green can you see? How does the ground feel under your feet – stones, grass, earth...? This is where I got the Tube sounds and sensations idea from. You can employ this kind of 'awareness of the senses' mindfulness practice wherever you are – provided it's safe to do so.

What things do you do in your day into which you could incorporate mindfulness? Boil a kettle? Pour a coffee? Read a book? Fall asleep? If you're new to the concept of self-awareness and you're not yet ready to dive into seeking laser-precision feedback about your behaviour from five colleagues, then being mindful is a good place to start. Creating your own internal feedback loop is personal, controllable and might shine a light on some interesting feedback that you don't have to share with anyone else.

Tests, Tools and Assessments

There are a huge number of tests, tools and assessments to help you uncover your strengths, values, gaps, preferences and biases. There are academically tested ones, socially tested ones, ones that are a bit of fun and ones that are deadly serious. A variety of techniques have been developed in the psychological sciences to measure soft and relational skills, like psychometrics, econometrics and psychophysics.[1] There is also quite a debate raging within academia as to whether it is appropriate to be measuring relational skills with hard measures at all. Many academics are highly critical of the preoccupation with quantitative research in the social sciences:[2] "How can an attribute that is constructed by humans be a quantity, or a real property at all?"[3] Well, yes, they've got a point. If a human attribute is not quantitative, then it can't really be measured, can it?[4]

Some scholars are of the view that to justify the use of measurement scales in psychology, psychometrics would need to comply with the formal framework of measurement in physics. But this would be impossible because mental attributes like self-awareness and emotional intelligence "are not as easy to handle and control as attributes are in physics".[5] Helpfully though, Pythagoras said that all things are made of numbers, and quantity and numbers are "ubiquitous features of every real situation".[6] This means we can express human thoughts and feelings through giving things numbers (i.e. enumerators) in a scale, which puts things that don't have standard measurements in order (i.e. ordinal scales). Here's an example of how enumerators can be used for measuring relational skills along an ordinal scale:

My manager is caring								
1	**2**	**3**	**4**	**5**	**6**	**7**	**8**	**9**
Uncaring (most negative)								Caring (most positive)
Please indicate where you feel your manager sits along this spectrum from most negative to most positive in relation to this statement: 1 is most in disagreement and 9 is most in agreement. 5 is your neutral point								

We know that caring is neither 35mm long nor 135mph fast; however, when you create an ordinal scale and give 'level of care' a number, you create a tool by which to measure care. You'll have had many experiences of completing this kind of questionnaire without giving the scaling much thought. Psychometric tests should be considered ordinal scaling, not measurement tools.[7] Here are some of the self-awareness/emotional intelligence tools mentioned in the literature that you may want to search out and complete for yourself or explore for your team or organisation.

The EQ:i[8] is one of the most widely used emotional intelligence measures and has 133 questions, assessing a variety of traits and self-concepts across the areas of intrapersonal, interpersonal, adaptability and stress management.[9] The EQ-i:S is the shorter little sibling, with 51 questions assessing intrapersonal, interpersonal, stress management, adaptability, general mood and positive impression.

The trait meta-mood scale (TMMS)[10] has 30 questions, assessing attention to change in one's mood, discerning the causes of change in one's mood and regulating one's mood. The trait emotional intelligence questionnaire short form (TEIQue-SF)[11] has 30 questions assessing a general measure of global emotional intelligence.

Here are some of the popular leader effectiveness measurement tools: the Multifactor Leadership Questionnaire (MLQ)[12] and its short form (45 questions), the MLQ-5X,[13] is the most popular instrument for measuring transformational and transactional leadership.[14] It includes different versions so that you can assess yourself and others can assess you. The Authentic Leadership Questionnaire[15] has 16 questions about "relational transparency, internal moral perspective, balanced processing and self-awareness".[16]

The Resonant Leadership Scale,[17] the one I used in my research, has its foundations in Canada's healthcare sector.[18] In Part 2, the section on leadership explored resonant leadership, which is founded on emotional intelligence. Being that emotional intelligence is frequently used interchangeably with self-awareness, this might be a tool you want to find out more about. It uses a five-point Likert scale where participants indicate the extent to which they feel their immediate supervisor displays particular types of leadership behaviours.[19] It too has got an 'I assess me' and 'you assess me' version of the questionnaire.

There are also numerous other tools, tests and assessments to help you increase your self-awareness: Myers-Briggs Type Indicator personality type (MBTI); Kolb's learning style test; Strengths Finder 2.0; Honey and Mumford learning styles; DISC (Dominance, Influence, Steadiness and Conscientiousness); the Enneagram; Leadership Circle Profile 360° Assessment; Insights; 16 Personality Factor (PF); Team Management Profile – TMSDI; Hogan Assessment; Red Bull Wingfinger; etc.

If you're looking for robust evidence of effectiveness, look these tools up on Google's academic search facility, Google Scholar.

There are also numerous tests, tools and assessments linked to professional development books, for example:

- Find out if you're currently blooming, budding, stunted or in need of renewal through the Work-Life Bloom Personal Assessment by Dan Pontefract, linked to his book *Work-Life Bloom*. (You can find links in The Back Pages.)

- The LEAD. CARE. WIN. assessment helps determine your leadership behaviour against the nine areas of focus in Dan Pontefract's book *Lead. Care. Win.*

- The Ally Mindset Profile by Morag Barrett, Eric Spencer and Ruby Vesely evaluates your strengths and potential areas for improvement in the five essential practices that create ally relationships, linked to their book, *You, Me, We.*

- The Deep Listening Quiz by Oscar Trimboli helps you identify your listening villains and provides you with a clear understanding of your number one listening barrier, linked to his book *Deep Listening*.

- The Daring Leadership Assessment by Brené Brown helps you gauge your strengths and your opportunities for growth as a daring leader, linked to her book *Dare to Lead*.

- The Wholehearted Inventory instrument by Brené Brown assesses your strengths and opportunities for growth, linked to her book *The Gifts of Imperfection*.

- The FABS Leadership Assessment by Robert Jordan and Olivia Wagner assesses your leadership style (fixer, artist, builder, strategist), linked to their book *Right Leader, Right Time*.

- The EGG3 Leadership Assessment by Ian Hatton and the team at Totally Morpheus assesses current leadership state, leadership values and leadership focus (individual, team, transformational and self-leadership).

Use these tests, tools and assessments as helpful guides on your journey along your superhighway. They won't be a panacea and obliterate your blind spot. They'll be a good update for your satnav. And when you build new junctions, connections, roundabouts and roadways on your superhighway, you will need to complete them again or find newly developed ones. They will undoubtedly tell you things you knew about yourself, present you with an infographic of yourself that you never imagined or unearth things you never knew were there. They're useful and helpful, and I highly recommend them as a wing mirror for the soul and a reflection on the self.

Journaling

Journaling is a very effective way to give you an opportunity to collect your thoughts and also give you the distance from them to observe, reflect on, critique, advise and change them in the future. In *The No Bullsh*t Guide to a Happier Life* podcast hosted by Helen Calvert, in the episode 'Journaling | The No Bullsh*t Guide to Journaling', she says it's a great tool for quietening the carnival of her crazy mind. If you've got a lot going on inside your head, journaling can be a good way to get it all out, park it all and then start moving those crazy bumper cars into their designated parking spaces to help you make sense of your experiences and thoughts, facilitating action planning and decision making. Take a listen to this episode. It's good.

Like other tools and techniques to generate greater self-awareness, journaling has a spectrum from internal to external. Journaling at the internal end of the spectrum takes the general form of writing down what's happened during the day, the week, the particular instance or the end of a time period that suits you. There are no hard and fast rules to journaling, and it should simply fit your routine and align with your needs. You may find that daily journaling serves you better, or it may be that once in a while is okay for you. But it's worth noting that, just like meditation, practice means that journaling is a skill you hone, and doing it when you want it but don't need it means it's more accessible to you when you need it but don't want it.

What might you focus on within your journaling? Would you focus on what happened during your day? Would you write about your feelings over a week, or maybe behaviour, or your interactions with others? You might want to capture all these things. You might give yourself a time limit of ten minutes; you might decide it's something you do before breakfast or before bedtime. As with all things human, a structure and a routine is best, so try it out. Test out the routine, juggle it around and see what lands into your life the best. Journaling can be as little or as large as you like. You could write a 300-word reflection at the end of every month, or you could write a 1,000-word reflection at the end of every day. The decision is entirely yours.

When I moved from Wales to England in 2019, I purged my bookshelves and put into storage that which didn't go to the charity shop. I thought I might go digital, but it turns out I quite like a real book and the smell of paper. In my house right now, I have two journals. One is a learning journal developed by Public Service Management Wales, the precursor to Academi Wales. I've always loved this journal. To start, it's a solid little A5 book in a beautiful purple. Every page has a template asking, What happened? Describe the incident/learning experience. How well did it go, and how do I feel about it? What have I learnt? How will I use this learning in future? They're helpful questions to focus the mind on particular situations and are simple enough for you to answer in your own context.

The other journal I have is *Your Prescription for Wellbeing Journal* by Alison Smith. Its aim is to help you work through stuck-ness. The structured template encourages you to think about symptoms, sayings you use to describe the situation, things you can do that help, things you do that don't help and who you could talk to about this. This focus on stuck-ness means this journal allows you to be your own coach. Get all the thoughts out of your head, put them down and use what you wrote to coach yourself in another situation. If you're in a stuck place, I'd highly recommend Alison's book *Can't See the Wood for the Trees? Landscaping Your Life to Get Back on Track*. It will resonate with you even more if you like the outdoors and appreciate the healing benefits of being in green spaces or near water. You can also listen to Alison on my podcast (episode 4).

When I spoke to Carly Cannings (episode 27), she told me she journals in the third person, which you may want to explore as an alternative to the first person. Carly talked about the importance of avoiding self-criticism and finding a way to reflect on your work, your communication and your behaviour objectively. She also said that employing the 'friend test' is a good way to approach self-reflection – 'What would you say to a good friend in the same situation?' It's a helpful way of reflecting on your practice with kindness and empathy. Try journaling in the third person as a way of giving yourself greater distance, perspective and objectivity.

We all like picking faults with others and feeding the little demon voice on our shoulder that tells us so-and-so was in the wrong, so-and-so really wasn't very good at that. Did you see what so-and-so was wearing?? What if you used journaling to help change your reflective perspective from the inside looking out to the outside looking in? How would that feel? What words would you use to describe yourself? What would you observe and write down about your communication style, your language and your behaviour?

Andrew Bryant (episode 44) told me about how he'd used journaling to reframe his perspective. He'd decided to give up alcohol and wrote it down in his journal. However, re-reading what he'd written made him feel like he'd 'given something up', which wasn't a good feeling. Andrew reflected on what he was getting in return: better sleep, weight loss and a reduction in acid reflux. The act of journaling had functioned as a self-coaching exercise, and Andrew was able to move into a far more positive mindset. This example takes journaling from being an activity that allows you to get the thoughts from inside your head onto the page to being one that enables you to constructively change the thoughts on paper and filter them back into your mind in a far more positive frame. You can read more about Andrew's thoughts on journaling in his book – full details in The Back Pages.

I've also discovered 'FutureMe letters' via a website called FutureMe. org. You can send an email to yourself six months, one year, three years, five years and ten years into the future. It might not fit strictly under the heading of journaling; maybe it's something more aligned to gratefulness and self-care, but because it involves getting the ideas out of your head down onto a page, there are similarities. Think of it like a personalised digital time capsule, where you can set out what's happening in your life right now and your wishes and aspirations for yourself in the future. If imposter syndrome is something you battle with, a little bit of self-

"Be careful what you say to yourself because you are listening."

Lisa M. Hayes

coaching, self-praise and self-love through these future letters can be really powerful. They can be a good reminder that you are good enough and you are doing your best. I've received an email from myself following a one-year gap, and it was incredibly emotional – a real self-esteem booster.

"Be careful what you say to yourself because you are listening."
Lisa M. Hayes

Another way of journaling, but with an outward focus rather than inward reflection, is to consider what you're grateful for. A gratitude board, list, wall of Post-it notes or virtual whiteboard – whatever you choose to use – has the potential to allow you to reflect as an individual or a collective. The beauty of collective reflection on things you're grateful for is that it sets a tone of what your collective considers important. This is equally true for families as it is for workplaces. We know from earlier discussion that the true values of an organisation aren't the things written in the corporate strategy; they're the behaviours you model and reward in your organisation. A regular reflection exercise focussed on gratitude is a clear and transparent articulation of exactly what you value. If a corporate strategy sets out professionalism as a value, then gratitude for problem solving will be congruous. If a corporate strategy sets out care as a value, then gratitude for the colleague who resigned when they got sick is incongruous.

To accompany you on your journey, get hold of a copy of *The Self-Awareness Superhighway Reflections Journal*, available to buy from my website, ksko.co.uk. Every entry gives you the opportunity to score your behaviour against a nine-point Likert scale, where nine is the most positive, one is the most negative and five is the neutral middle. You score your behaviour on a radar graph and join the dots to create your superhighway map. The compass points with the lowest scores are the ones you need to focus more on in your journey along your Self-Awareness Superhighway.

Alongside every score, you have an opportunity to note your thoughts, observations and reflections related to those scores. Consider noting down reflections on your hard and relational skills, recognition of your impact on others and how you intend to regulate your behaviour next time. You can journal daily, weekly or simply when the mood takes you, but as mentioned above, consistency builds mastery.

Below is an example of how a reflection chart might look. The lines on your map show you the direction you need to focus your attention.

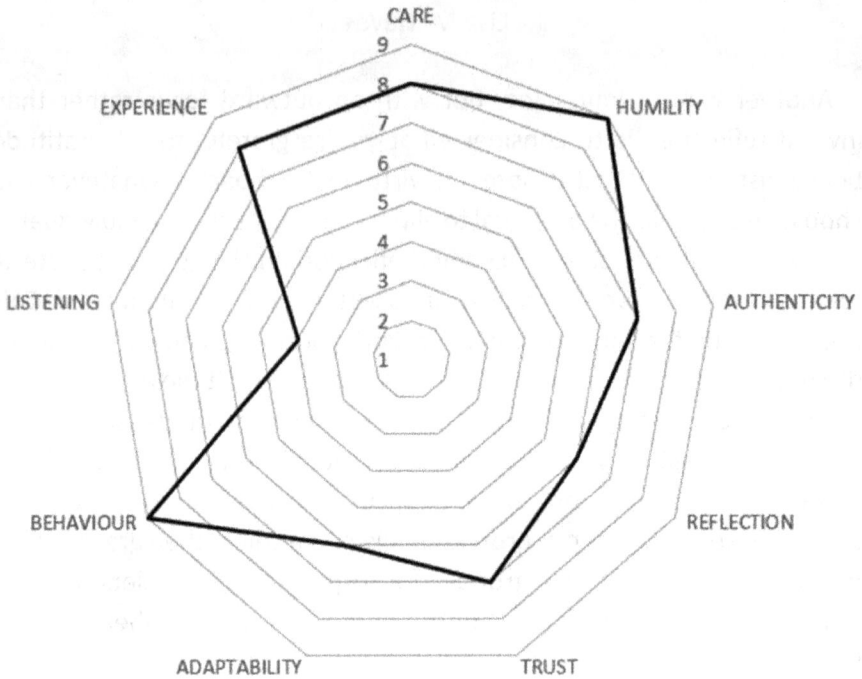

In this example, listening is a behaviour that needs greater focus. Go back to the tests, tools and assessments section to identify the tool that would be most helpful to you in exploring listening and use the findings to help you chart your Self-Awareness Superhighway map and development action plan towards listening. Modelling behaviour and humility are directions well travelled.

Details on where you can get hold of the journal can be found in The Back Pages.

Coaching and Mentoring

Over the last 20 years, coaching and mentoring have been gaining a foothold in the core list of leadership development tools. *Many Knowing Self Knowing Others Podcast* guests have talked about coaching, many because they are professional coaches and can extol the benefits of it from experience.

Coaches come from both inside and outside organisations. The relationship between line managers and direct reports should include elements of coaching and mentoring. Whether you're in a position of managing talent or managing poor performance, the same should be true. Your monthly, bi-monthly or quarterly supervision sessions should coach strengths and mentor weaknesses. The weighting towards coaching or mentoring will be unique to every direct report.

Coaches who are inside your organisation but work in a different department bring a greater level of objectivity to the relationship than if they were from within your department – and knew where all the bodies are buried. Being that there are cultures operating within cultures in big organisations, one department can feel and operate quite differently to another. That means a coach from a different department can bring different experiences and perspectives to your discussion.

External coaches are often brought in from people development companies. They don't need to know your area of expertise, but they do need to be adept at listening, skilled in reflecting your words back to you, accomplished in summarising your discussion and effective in holding you to account for actioning your decisions.

Mentors, on the other hand, are often people who have some greater or lesser degree of knowledge about your professional area of work, organisation or world in general. This is helpful in that they can share their experiences and you can learn from them in a more specific and direct way.

Coaching and mentoring have benefits for colleagues from all levels of the FFJLF: operational, business, management, senior management and strategic. As mentioned earlier, Dr Gerrit Pelzer (episode 22) said coaching is often put in place for people at the top of organisations because that's where the biggest bang for their buck is presumed to be. But if you consider that leaders can be found at all levels of organisations, then coaching has the potential to be useful to anybody and is certainly something to consider when you're succession planning. For people at the middle and lower levels of organisations, coaching and mentoring opens up the potential to explore tasks, relationships, red tape and all the other wicked workplace challenges from a different perspective. Managers and leaders frequently appoint in their likeness, meaning that cognitive diversity is often lacking within teams, so an external coach or mentor can be extremely helpful.

For senior and strategic employees, external coaches and mentors have the potential to provide the perspective that internal colleagues can't. You'll read more about that in a little while, when you get to 'filtered feedback'. An external coach or mentor is not paid or beholden to senior leaders in the same way that internal employees are, giving them the ability to operate with a greater level of candour than people on the inside. This makes them very valuable resources to senior management and strategic-level employees who have a genuine interest in developing their self-awareness and becoming better leaders. For those who don't, of course, they're likely to be real pains in the arse. But when organisations are looking to make a pre-emptive self-awareness reveal on the inside before an employee becomes a liability and a million-pound lawsuit on the outside, then endured the pain must be!

When I talked to Síle Walsh (episode 14), who has a background in coaching psychology and organisational development, I asked her about where self-awareness fits in the coaching journey. She told me that coaching is about change. You don't need to have self-awareness to come to coaching. What you do need is readiness for change. With a desire to change comes a desire to develop and grow, and to do that effectively, you have to start the journey by raising self-awareness. We all have blind spots, and coaching can bring those areas into the light. Once the light has been switched on, Síle said it's then that the work of coaching really starts.

How can *you* capitalise on coaching and mentoring? Lots of organisations will already have opportunities in place for you to seek out a coach or a mentor. You may have people in your organisation who are putting out feelers for coachees or mentees to work with to give them the practice hours they need for their training course. If, however, the offers in your organisation aren't obvious or don't exist, have a discussion with your line manager and ensure your discussion is recorded. They or you can then make contact with your organisational development (OD) department to either explore what's on offer or put something in place. If you work in a smaller organisation, there may be opportunities to talk to your external human resources provider to see what OD functions they can offer or broker. Failing that, put a call out on LinkedIn for recommendations.

You may be a line manager, coach and mentor to your direct reports, but you're likely to be a direct report to someone else. That means the benefit of a coaching and/or mentoring relationship with your line manager should also be afforded to you. Do you feel cared for? Does your manager behave with humility and authenticity? Do they encourage you to reflect? Do they behave so as to build your trust? Are they adaptable? Do they model behaviour, listen and share their experiences with you through a coaching and mentoring approach? If they do, did this relationship develop organically, or was it something you discussed and constructively established? If they don't, can you instigate a conversation to develop the kind of relationship you need?

How can you build up your coaching and mentoring muscle? The best way to start is definitely to be coached and mentored. Get a sense of what it means for you. What kind of coach/mentor do you want to be? What kind of coach/mentor do you not want to be?! Consider doing a coaching or mentoring training course. There are lots of accredited bodies that now run professional training that encompasses both written and practical elements. Seek out a course that includes both, where you can reflect on your practice, discuss with a supervisor and set out your own plan for improvement and growth. Avoid the five-hour online course without any human interaction or critique of your practice and no supervision. If you're looking to become a coach, aim to do it with humility and integrity and model the behaviour you'd want to see in a coach and mentor. Whether your intention is to offer coaching or mentoring more formally or to provide a better experience to your direct reports, a coaching or mentoring course will help you become a more active listener and learn to ask better questions.

Feedback

The thing with feedback is that it's going to find you, eventually, so you're better off inviting it in rather than waiting for it to creep up on you. That feedback juggernaut is going to pass you on your superhighway at some point, so you can either ride with your back to the oncoming traffic and hope it doesn't squash you, or you can fit some wing mirrors to your scooter and pull off into the service station to deal with the dust it throws up.

You need to have three mirrors on each side:

- One that tells you what's coming, because you can always see behind you out of the corner of your eye, i.e. build your reflective practice into a business-as-usual activity that's always in your line of sight.

- One that your pillion passenger can see into so they can tap you on the shoulder when they see that juggernaut coming, i.e. find people who've got your back and will draw your awareness to your behaviour when they need to.

- And a third mirror you can glance into once in a while for extra reassurance, i.e. extra processes like 360-degree reviews supplement your self-awareness journey; it's the third mirror that provides you with a life-saver glance.

When you seek feedback, do it with integrity. If you ask for feedback when you don't really want to receive it, people will smell it a mile off. If people are brave enough to tell you the truth that you don't want to hear, you're setting them up to be in your firing line forevermore. Organisational leaders need to develop psychological safety and open the door to candour. Passive openness to feedback won't develop self-aware leadership like actively seeking it out will. As a leader, be genuine in your quest for feedback! Wise words from Liam Maguire (episode 19).

You have to ensure you ask for and receive feedback from the right people. If you take on board the verbal and non-verbal feedback everyone is giving you all the time, you'll drive yourself crazy. Be discerning as to who you seek feedback from. The golden rule is to only accept feedback from people whose opinions you respect. Because haters gonna hate! Jealousy is often a catalyst for vicious feedback. You want to hear feedback from those who would sit pillion on your scooter and check out your second mirror for approaching juggernauts.

In her book *Insight*, which is all about developing self-awareness, Dr Tasha Eurich recommends feedforward, not feedback. Feedback tells you about a past you can't change. Feedforward tells you about what you can do better next time. Sally Evans (episode 2) and I talked about using 'what' to develop your self-awareness. Rather than getting feedback on "How did I do?", start asking, "What can I do differently? What can I do to help you? What can I do more of?" These questions draw out far more useful and practical advice.

The biggest barrier to effective feedback is 'filtered feedback'. The more senior you are, the more obscured your view is and the more hazy your vision down to the furthest reaches of your organisation. Matthew Phelan (episode 13) said that when you're the one paying the wages, feedback will always be filtered. There is a concept called the Iceberg of Ignorance, developed in 1989 by Sidney Yoshida, that says executives see 4% of the problems, team managers see 9% of the problems, team leaders see 74% and staff see 100%. That means 96% of problems are hidden from senior management.

Joanna Rawbone (episode 6) and I talked about the damage created when leaders surround themselves with people who are 'like them' in a space where they aren't afforded the safety to speak up. When that happens, an echo chamber is created and a leader's behaviour is echoed back to them, reinforcing it, setting the standard for the organisation and, ultimately, creating the organisation's culture. This is a clear indication that senior recruitment needs a shake-up, and cognitive diversity around the leader needs to be improved to make sure filtering doesn't become censorship and feedback doesn't become a feeble or, worse still, strong echo.

If you think back over your career and your behaviour towards senior people, I'm sure you'll recall times when you've laughed at unfunny jokes and said yeeees to things when the real answer was noooooo. It's self-preservation. I certainly know I've said, "Excellent!" when what I really thought was *That's going to go down like a lead balloon!* But like a good little foot-soldier, I sucked it up because my need to pay my mortgage was greater than my desire to be the one to tell the boss this just wasn't going to work. Chief happiness officer and founder of Happy Coffee Consulting Sarah Metcalfe (episode 1) likened it to the dilemma in the story of 'The Emperor's New Clothes'. No one wants to be the one to point out the lack of substance in the boss's new threads!

Jon Rennie (episode 11) said leaders need to move around their company to get the reality check they need. Jon does 'Fridays on the floor' – when he and his senior team go out into the open environment of his production company and talk to people to find out how things are going. It's a very practical way to get feedback about how people are feeling, what's being done, how it's being done and what people need. How visible are you to your operational staff, and how much time do you spend with them?

If you're a manager of people as well as a person who's being 'managed', you have to be a part of making sure echo chambers don't develop and be a giver of feedback and feedforward too. Little is discussed about how to seek feedback and feedforward or how to ask others how they want to receive it. If you give feedback in the way *you* like to receive it, you could end up turning a perfectly good relationship sour. If you're giving feedback upwards, this is the killer question you need an answer to: how does your manager want to receive feedback? Your continued employment might depend on it!

Feedback is one of the most discussed methods of building self-awareness on my podcast. Feedback is a gift if you're prepared to receive it, is Tracy Myhill's view (episode 18). You've got the potential to learn from it and be a better you than you were yesterday, if you choose to hear it. Other people's views are a tonic for the ego, is what Liam Maguire said (episode 19). Objective feedback can be difficult to hear but necessary if you really want to develop your self-aware leadership skills.

360-Degree Reviews

One of the best ways to overcome filtered feedback is to use a 360-degree review. They are based on an 'I rate me, you rate me' model, like the ones used in the self/other ratings studies. The 'others' who are usually invited to rate you tend to be two direct reports and one senior. If you've been given the chance to have five people rate you, you might go for three direct reports, a peer and a manager. If ten, then you scale it up. That sort of thing.

To do a full 360 properly, it's best to use someone who's accredited and trained to deliver that particular 360-degree assessment tool. A good process would be for the subject to give a facilitator up to 15 names of people in their direct report, peer and senior manager relationship groupings, for the facilitator to then randomly identify around three from each group, seek the feedback anonymously and analyse it before returning it to the rated individual as one aggregate report. There shouldn't be a time when the subject sees the individual scores given by individual people. If more raters have been used, maybe a report by relationship grouping would be possible, but scores shouldn't be identifiable and able to be linked to the people the subject initially listed. If an assessment is touted as being anonymous, then to maintain the integrity of the facilitator, fidelity of the tool and confidentiality of the rater, anonymity must be protected within the process. If anonymity isn't assured in a process where anonymity is promised, there is an increased likelihood of negative consequences to the honest rater.

Some organisations use 360s without a facilitator providing an intermediary buffer. The senior subject is given carte blanche to pick the subordinate raters, the number of raters is so small that they are identifiable through the law of averages, and all the feedback received is 'good, excellent, glowing, awesome and fabulous'. A real waste of time and energy. What would you learn from that, other than your organisation is half-heartedly implementing a tried-and-tested development tool, lip service is being given to the development of self-aware leadership and staff generally feel unable to speak up?

"To be self-aware, you need to acquire a birds-eye view of yourself – to experience yourself from the outside."
Amy Gandon, episode 15

Dr Gerrit Pelzer and Martin Aldergard host *Second Crack – The Leadership Podcast*. In episode 25, '360-Degree Feedback: A Welcome Punch in the Gut for Leaders', Gerrit and Martin talk about the benefits and challenges of 360s, including how people can be defensive in their receipt of the feedback. Even if the subject perceives it as 'explaining' the feedback given, it's received as defensiveness. They suggest that involvement in designing the 360 process helps to prepare the ground for receiving feedback. This aligns with what I've talked about in this book about inclusive decision making. The notion is applicable in many contexts.

Formal acknowledgement from the subject and giving thanks to the raters is also something to consider. Formal acknowledgement of 'I've had your feedback, I've heard your feedback, and I'm learning from your feedback' would create a sense of authenticity, humility and vulnerability, which would be good for morale and culture. If you're a part of a 360 or responsible for putting one in motion in your organisation, maybe this is something you could consider as a requirement. Perhaps the facilitator could draw out elements of learning for the subject to consider feeding back to their raters as an acknowledgement of their contribution and value to you. It also models the behaviour you'd want to see, reinforces the importance of feedback and perpetuates psychological safety within the organisation.

After being in a new role for six months, I carried out a feedforward exercise. I wouldn't call it a 360 as it didn't have all the elements required. I sought anonymised feedback/forward from my direct reports, peers and line manager by asking these questions. You might consider posing them to trusted colleagues and formulating a way for them to respond anonymously. You could also put them to your line manager, if these aren't already things they share with you.

1. What is something I already do now that you would like me to do more of in the future?

2. What is something I do now that you would like me to do less of in the future?

3. What do I do now that you would like me to do differently in the future?

4. What could I do to be more helpful or supportive of you/you and your team?

If you want to develop your self-awareness and generate a culture of self-aware leadership in your organisation, these exercises matter. If you model the behaviour you want to see, then you're going to want people seeing you very publicly seeking out feedback. If you have someone on your team who isn't self-aware enough, you as the leader need to go first and seek out feedback and be seen to be seeking out feedback. Demonstrate that you're aware you have a natural, human blind spot and you're seeking to shine a light on it.

You have to lead the way, in all ways.

The Self-Awareness Compass Quiz

One of the important things I want to give you as part of this book is a tool to help you decide which compass directions to follow. When you are charting your map along your superhighway, where should you go? To help you find out, I've developed a self/other rating quiz for you – The Self-Awareness Compass Quiz. Being that self-aware leadership is socially constructed, you can't decide if you are a self-aware leader without help from others. You can certainly decide to *be* a self-aware leader on your own, but in deciding whether you *are* one, that takes a little help from your friends... and colleagues!

The quiz has two parts. The first part is your self-assessment. You will be asked to assess yourself against each of the nine compass points. Each point will have a statement you will rate yourself against, e.g. I am caring, I am humble, I am authentic. You will be asked to rate yourself on a nine-point Likert scale, where one is 'most in disagreement' and nine is 'most in agreement'.

For example, let's take the statement, 'I am caring'. I think I'm fairly caring; I don't think I'm generally mean, but there are times when I could probably show more care, so I would rate myself a seven out of nine.

Let's take the statement, 'I am humble.' I'm quite humble because I don't generally offer opinions without being asked for them (introvert alert!), but sometimes my opinions burst out when I'm really frustrated, so I would rate myself an eight out of nine!

Five should be considered the neutral point. If I'd picked four, I would be rating myself as a bit uncaring and a bit boastful at times. If I'd rated myself a two, I'd definitely need to work on caring for others and spend more time travelling in the compass direction of care.

I am caring								
1	2	3	4	5	6	7	8	9
						X		

Please rate your agreement to this statement.

1 is most in disagreement and 9 is most in agreement. 5 is your neutral point.

I am humble								
1	2	3	4	5	6	7	8	9
							X	

Please rate your agreement to this statement.

1 is most in disagreement and 9 is most in agreement. 5 is your neutral point.

The second part is your 'others' assessment.

The Self-Awareness Compass Quiz gives you an opportunity to get some feedback from other people. You can share the quiz with up to three people who you would like to rate you. There is also a paid option to extend this to up to ten people. Your raters will receive an email asking them to rate you against the same nine compass points, on the same nine-point Likert scale, in response to the statements '[Your name] is caring, [Your name] is humble, [Your name] is trustworthy', etc.

Their version of the quiz will look like this...

Joe is caring								
1	**2**	**3**	**4**	**5**	**6**	**7**	**8**	**9**
							X	

Please rate your agreement to this statement.

1 is most in disagreement and 9 is most in agreement. 5 is your neutral point.

Joe is humble								
1	**2**	**3**	**4**	**5**	**6**	**7**	**8**	**9**
			X					

Please rate your agreement to this statement.

1 is most in disagreement and 9 is most in agreement. 5 is your neutral point.

Your other-raters will have a seven-day window to complete the quiz. At the end of the seven days, the quiz will close and you will be able to access your report identifying your scores.

Your scores will be made up of your self-ratings and the average of the scores given by your three raters to ensure they can't be identified. The Quiz is grounded in the 360-degree assessment idea and rather than using a facilitator, being that it's an online quiz, it aggregates your 'others rating' so as to anonymise your raters.

Your Self-Awareness Compass Quiz feedback might look something like this:

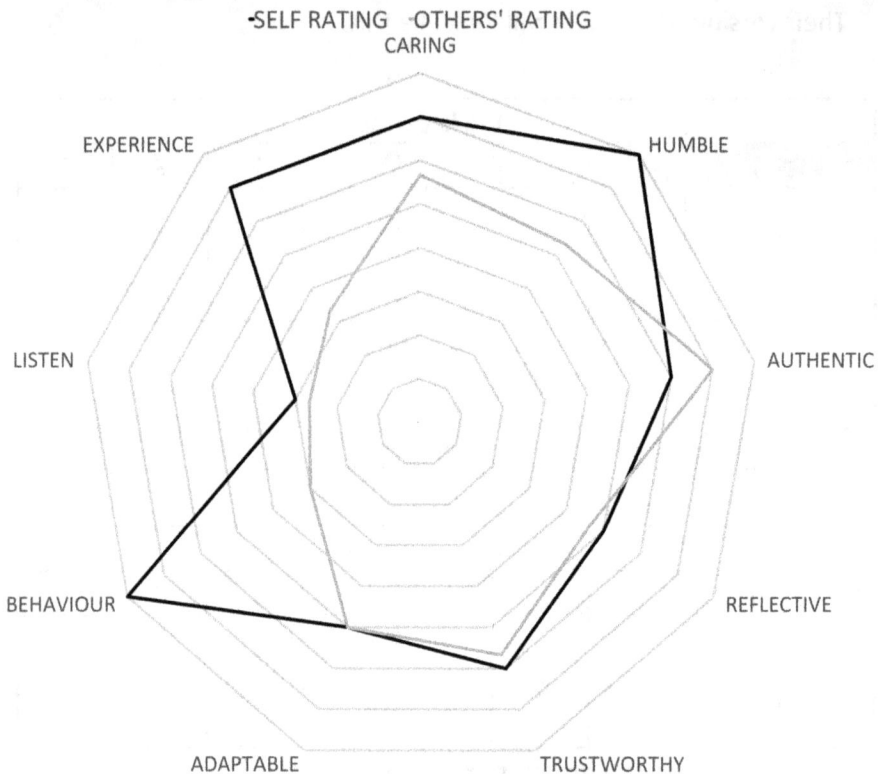

If you reflect on the ratings of the above map, your view of yourself and others' view of you are quite similar. Reflection, trust, adaptability and listening have been scored the same by all parties. Authenticity is a little different but in a positive way: others think you are more authentic than you do. This incongruity is something you will want to explore, but due to the positive discrepancy, you can set this down as something to explore at a later time.

Your self-rating suggests you think humility is one of your strengths; however, your raters don't view humility as being as strong a strength as you do. The same can be said for behaviour. Your ratings suggest you feel that you model behaviour well and view behaviour as one of your top strengths, along with humility. However, your raters seem to be in general disagreement with you. Both your self-rating and others' rating identify that listening is a skill you need to strengthen.

First, focus on listening, then behaviour, humility, learning from experience and caring, in that order.

Given what you've read about these five key components of self-aware leadership in Part 2, what can you do to improve your skills and to seek feedback from others to improve in these areas? What can you do to understand this incongruity? Take each of the five compass directions in turn and develop one or two clear, concrete and achievable actions to work on. If you have a positive and constructive relationship with your line manager, you could include them in charting your map and also holding you to account for spending more time in the land of listening, the bay of behaviour and the hills of humility. Otherwise, you could explore these areas with your coach or mentor.

In 6 to 12 months' time, revisit your Self-Awareness Compass Quiz and re-do it to evidence your progress. You could approach the same raters as before, or you could approach a different set of raters. If you recall, when you explored the definition of self-awareness, the self/other ratings studies found that others' ratings often had a greater degree of similarity between them than self and other. If you asked ten people the same questions, they'd probably all come back and say you needed to improve your listening skills to a greater or lesser extent, so don't worry about going back to the same people to re-do the quiz if it's not practical. If they've left the organisation where you did the first quiz, all is not lost. You will learn something every time you do the quiz.

Head to www.ksko.co.uk/quiz.

In the Rear-View Mirror

You started Part 3 of this book by contemplating the question, 'How will you get there?', and you've come to the end of the exploration of your travel guide. You've journeyed through mindfulness and meditation as ways to calm your thinking, get to know your inner self, count up mindful minutes and assess your LPA. You've explored a range of tests, tools and assessments available to help you gauge your preferences. Some are academically tested, some are socially researched and some are a bit of fun. You considered journaling as a way of transferring thoughts onto a page to unburden yourself from them and to give you distance and the opportunity to identify behaviour patterns. You were also introduced to *The Self-Awareness Superhighway Reflections Journal*, which is available to accompany this book. You can use it as a tool to help reflect on your self-aware leadership journey along your superhighway whilst helping to direct your journey's next leg.

You have explored coaching and mentoring as ways of enlisting others to support you in charting your map, considering the benefits of providing coaching and mentoring to leaders at all levels, not just the strategic level. You've dived into the uncertain world of feedback, acknowledging that seeking it out is a better strategy than waiting for it to run you over like a runaway juggernaut. You've trudged up the hill of filtered feedback and recognised the challenge strategic-level leaders have in mitigating against that filtration whilst also bridging the gap between the factory floor and the top of the iceberg. You've rested at the service station to admire the beauty of the 360-degree assessment rainbow and acknowledge that many a rainbow comes after a storm. Finally, you've taken a whistle-stop tour through the Self-Awareness Compass Quiz, which I give to you with heartfelt excitement in the hope that it will help you on your self-aware leadership journey, giving you the information you need to chart your future superhighway map.

9. ARRIVALS

Self-aware leadership is a lifelong journey that doesn't end until you reach your final departure gate and pop off this mortal coil. Every stop in between is an arrival from one place and a transfer lounge to another. You and I have reached our arrivals terminal together, and now you have the fun of looking through your travel snaps and reflecting on your journey before you move on into the transfer lounge and head off on your next big adventure.

Why You Are Here

Part 1 set out the definitions and descriptions to help you answer the question, why are you here, traveller? You discovered the importance of self-awareness, leader effectiveness and leadership at all levels to you as an individual and those around you.

You explored the history of self-awareness from the Socratic wisdom of 'Know thyself' to the modern-day definition used in this book, distilled to 'reflection, recognition and regulation'. We discussed the self/other ratings studies as the seminal work and academic anchors for the topic of self-aware leadership, which is very much interested in individuals operating at the top of organisations, using a 360-degree review model to capture findings. You read about the connections between self-awareness and emotional intelligence and the interchangeability of the terms. You learnt about the differences between men and women and how followers rate the self-awareness of both. You also explored how introverts and extroverts think and talk, the extraversion bias and the power of quiet leaders.

You discovered the history of leadership research and the change in leadership trends over the century, from traits and characteristics to behaviours and styles. Together, we unpicked the terms hard skills and soft skills, preferring to refer to the latter as relational skills because they're anything but soft! To be effective, the weight of importance sits squarely on the side of relational skills, but hard skills are necessary for effectiveness too. You explored the power that leaders have just by walking into a room and the shadows leaders create within their organisations, whether they realise it or not. You heard about the views and thoughts shared by guests who joined me on *The Knowing Self Knowing Others Podcast*, testing the academic ideas in a real-world context. You considered nature and nurture and jumped off the fence with me into the field of nature whilst accepting that nature without nurture doesn't always a leader make!

You explored the FFJLF, which introduced a broadly applicable structure to different organisations to help you understand and compare them. The functional layers of strategic, senior management, management, business and operational were set out, helping you to frame your later travels through the book. You examined the traditional pyramid-shaped hierarchical structures of the industrial paradigm and the emerging interest in complex adaptive systems and complexity leadership, which is seemingly more geared towards the adaptability needed for the knowledge-based paradigm. You read about the traditional view of leadership linked to seniority and the more modern and emerging view of leadership at all levels. You explored the debate about leaders with titles and social leaders without and the impact of influence as a leadership skill, regardless of your level within the organisational hierarchy.

I set out a clear three-layer definition of self-aware leadership, taking into account internal self-awareness, internal-social self-awareness, external-social self-awareness, hard skills and relational skills, articulating it simply as...

**reflection of hard skills and relational skills,
recognition of impact and regulation of behaviour.**

In the transfer lounge of Part 1, I asked you why you were here, traveller? Reflect on the answers you gave to see how far you've come. Has your journey through this book provided you with the answers for your onward journey on your Self-Awareness Superhighway?

Where You Are Going

In Part 2 you explored the question, where are you going?, by discovering the nine directions of the self-aware leadership compass. Your journey was enabled by signposts and directions and then disrupted by roadblocks and trip hazards. You explored the nine CHARTABLE compass points of care, humility, authenticity, reflection, trust, adaptability, behaviour, listening and experience. You reconnoitred each direction, discovering the thoughts, ideas, experiences and wisdom from my many podcast guests to bring the realities of the world of work into vivid view.

The journey exploring the enabling signposts and directions began with strategy and headed to planning and organisational standards as the foundations from which all other organisational decisions spring. You travelled around the planes of people management, exploring recruitment, supervision, performance reviews, organisational development and wellbeing. You considered the discussion about the importance of individuals operating together as strong teams and the benefit of robust peer relationships. You also read about the challenges and benefits of living and working in the same community and the need for organisations to recognise the inextricability of personal and professional life for many people. You ended the chapter by finding out more about the clear benefits of inclusive decision making as a bridge over the ravine of strategic-level disconnect.

Part 2 concluded by exploring the disabling roadblocks and trip hazards that you need to be aware of and mitigate against and, if all else fails, simply manoeuvre around. You explored the challenge of disconnection and detachment between strategic and operational-level employees and the need to lean heavily on inclusive decision making to traverse the ravine. You read about the restrictions of red tape and bureaucracy, slowing organisations down and making them unresponsive and cumbersome, whilst recognising that in some organisations, people have learnt to work around processes to become more agile. You explored crises, stress and their physiological impacts on individuals, considering Covid and climate change as wake-up calls for the need to be better prepared, more agile and more adept at managing black swan events. You explored psychological toxicity as the antithesis to psychological safety, delving into topics such as the Speak Up movement, incivility and disrespect, recognising the damage even micro-incivilities can have on individuals, particularly those in your care. You ended Part 2 with a discussion about accidental leaders: technical experts promoted into people management roles through the false view that expertise in hard skills leads to an innate expertise in people management.

How You Will Get There

Part 3 gave you the tools and techniques for your journey along your unique Self-Awareness Superhighway. You began by exploring mindfulness and meditation as methods to pause your external world and focus on introspection for a healthy mind and body, building your resilience and ability to cope with the roadblocks and trip hazards of the world of work. You read about its benefit as a tool to use any time, any place, anywhere – no expensive trainers required.

You explored the myriad tests, tools and assessments available to you to help identify your preferences, expose your strengths and uncover your weaknesses. You considered academic tools and social tools, all of which function like little rear-view mirrors, helping you minimise your blind spot and giving you a better view of yourself as others might see you. A helpful list of tests, tools and assessments is included in the chapter for you.

You took a tour through journaling as a way of getting your thoughts out of your head and onto the page for better inspection, analysis and consideration, allowing you to take an objective step away and notice any trends, areas for growth and opportunities for reframing. You read about journaling in the third person as an approach to giving you greater distance and building your objectivity muscle.

You learnt about coaching and mentoring as methods to achieve greater objectivity with the help of others, considering the pros and cons of internal and external coaches and mentors. You also read about the benefits of coaching at all levels – a way of nurturing talent and providing benefits right across organisations, not merely the strategic top.

You dived into the intricacies of feedback, gaining awareness of the benefits of inviting it in rather than letting it knock you off your scooter. You read about the importance of seeking feedback with integrity and an intention to hear it and implement change. You considered the importance of seeking feedback from those people that have your back and of asking feedforward questions to discover what you can change rather than what you can't. You considered the challenge of filtered feedback and the need to be active in preventing the contagion of echo chambers.

You explored 360-degree reviews and the importance of good facilitation, analysis and feedback to benefit the self-subject and protect the other-raters. You received a few suggestions of the questions you could ask when seeking feedforward.

You concluded Part 3 with my gift to you – the Self-Awareness Compass Quiz, the assessment tool that allows you to rate your own behaviours against the nine directions of the self-awareness compass and invite feedback from friends, family and colleagues. Your quiz findings will help you action plan and chart a course for your onward journey along your Self-Awareness Superhighway.

And now our journey together is done.

You must pass through the transfer lounge and on to the next leg of your self-aware leadership journey along your superhighway. You may instantly know the direction you need to travel, or you may decide to stay in the transfer lounge, take the weight off, grab a coffee and reflect a little while longer. Whatever you decide to do and in whatever direction you decide to travel, this guide will be with you, the podcast will be accessible to you and the Self-Awareness Compass Quiz will be there for you to use and re-use.

I wish you bon voyage in developing your self-aware leadership and in developing other self-aware leaders around the globe to generate kinder, more respectful and creative working relationships through reflection, recognition and regulation.

I wish you a safe, long and fulfilling journey, traveller, and I hope our superhighways will cross again and we'll catch a glimpse of each other in our rear-view mirrors from time to time.

THE BACK PAGES

KNOWING SELF KNOWING OTHERS RESOURCES

Knowing Self Knowing Others Online

Website: www.ksko.co.uk

Blog: Access all of my blog posts via my website.

Social media: My website will take you to all of my social media accounts on LinkedIn, Instagram, Facebook, YouTube, TikTok, Substack, etc. You can also click on the link to my Linktree, which brings all my links together in one place.

Newsletter: You can sign up for my weekly podcast top takeaways newsletter and monthly reflections newsletter.

The Knowing Self Knowing Others Podcast

Audio: You can listen to the podcast on Apple Podcasts, Spotify, Amazon Music, Goodpods, Podchaser, Deezer, Listen Notes and more. By visiting my website and clicking on 'podcast' and 'listen', you can access it straight from your browser too.

Video: Many of my podcasts are now also available in video, along with audio on YouTube, which you can access via the little icons on the top right of my website.

Clips: Short video clips of top takeaways from podcast episodes can be found on TikTok and Instagram.

The Self-Awareness Superhighway Reflections Journal

www.ksko.co.uk/journal

The Self-Awareness Compass Quiz

www.ksko.co.uk/quiz

RECOMMENDED RESOURCES

Here are some helpful resources to keep you company on your self-aware leadership journey as you travel along your superhighway.

Podcasts

Deep Leadership by Jon Rennie

Finding Brave by Kathy Caprino

Geeks, Geezers and Googlization by Ira Wolfe and Jason Cochran

Happier at Work by Aoife O'Brien

Happiness and Humans by Matthew Phelan

Landscaping Your Life by Alison Smith

Leading by Rory Stewart and Alastair Campbell

Second Crack — The Leadership Podcast by Dr Gerrit Pelzer and Martin Aldergard

Secret Leaders by Dan Murray-Serter

Soft Skills for Leaders by Lisa Evans

The Centre for Army Leadership Podcast by The Centre for Army Leadership

The Culture Lab by Aga Bajer

The Flourishing Introvert Talks by Joanna Rawbone

The Happiness Lab by Pushkin and Dr Laurie Santos

The Leader Connect Podcast by Leader Connect and Neil Jurd

The Leadership Zone by Síle Walsh

The Quiet Warrior by Serena Low

Truth, Lies and Workplace Culture by Leanne Elliott and Al Elliott

WorkWell by Deloitte

Books

Begin With WE: 10 Principles for Building and Sustaining a Culture of Excellence by Kyle McDowell

Dare to Lead: Brave Work. Tough Conversations. Whole Hearts by Brené Brown

Insight: How to Succeed by Seeing Yourself Clearly by Dr Tasha Eurich

Jerks at Work: Toxic Coworkers and What To Do About Them by Tessa West

Leadership Is Language: The Hidden Power of What You Say and What You Don't by L. David Marquet

Quietly Powerful: How Your Quiet Nature Is Your Hidden Leadership Strength by Megumi Miki

Rebel Ideas: The Power of Thinking Differently by Matthew Syed

The Attributes: 25 Hidden Drivers of Optimal Performance by Rich Diviney

The Overthinker's Guide to Life by Andrew Sewell

Self-Leadership: How to Become a More Successful, Efficient, and Effective Leader from the Inside Out by Andrew Bryant and Ana Kazan

You, Me, We: Why We All Need a Friend at Work (and How to Show Up as One) by Morag Barrett, Eric Spencer and Ruby Vesely

ABOUT THE AUTHOR

Nia Thomas is an expert leader who talks the talk and walks the walk. She is an academically awarded researcher in self-aware leadership and practises self-aware leadership every single day in her role as a director of a children's charity.

Before moving to the charitable sector, Nia spent over 20 years working across the public sector in local government, the National Health Service and Civil Service, predominantly in Wales and, in the last few years, England.

Throughout her career, Nia has been interested in working relationships: the dynamics between people and the impact both good and bad relationships have on individuals, their wellbeing and ability to do their work. This led her to develop an interest in self-awareness, leader effectiveness and leadership at all levels, which became the focus of her doctoral research.

Nia was born and bred in St David's, the UK's smallest city, before moving to Cardiff for university. She spent a year in Japan during her undergraduate days and settled in Cardiff after graduation. She later moved north to the South Wales Valleys where she remained and made it her home. She met her husband through their shared love of cars, which is a passion they still enjoy. Together, they moved to London before the pandemic to pursue career opportunities.

Nia now lives in west Essex, within easy reach of London, where she loves to visit coffee shops and is on a mission to find the perfect gluten-free cake and the fanciest, tastiest ice cream – preferably both together!

You can find Nia at www.ksko.co.uk.

You can contact Nia by emailing info@ksko.co.uk.

ACKNOWLEDGEMENTS

With huge thanks to my research interviewees, who made my knowledge and understanding richer than I could ever imagine.

Thank you to the guests who joined me on *The Knowing Self Knowing Others Podcast* for their conversation, collaboration and continued connection. Thank you to each and every one who gave their permission to be included in this book: Alison Lagier, Alison Reynolds, Alison Smith, Amy Gandon, Amy Zhang, Anna Zannides, Andrew Bryant, Andrew Sewell, Carly Cannings, Chad Costa, Dan Pontefract, Donald Henderson, Dr Gerrit Pelzer, Gunther Verheyen, Ian Hatton, Ira S. Wolfe, Jacqui Frost, Jeroen Kraaijenbrink, Joanna Rawbone, Jon S. Rennie, Jonathan Wilson, Katrijn van Oudheusden, Dr Ketan Kulkarni, Kyle McDowell, Liam Maguire, Matt Stone JD, Matthew Phelan, Megumi Miki, Morag Barrett, Neil Jurd OBE, Nicki Eyre, Dr Reiner Kraft, Robert Jordan, Robertson Hunter Stewart, Sally Evans, Sarah Metcalfe, Sathpal Singh, Serena Low, Síle Walsh, Sophie Bryan, Stephen Shedletzky and Tracy Myhill OBE. I appreciate your insights and contribution to my learning journey.

A heartfelt thank you to my diligent beta readers, Emilia Piera, Tara Poore, Katharine Heeps and Michael Freeston, for doing what they said they'd do and providing constructive feedback that helped make this book into a gorgeous book.

With much love to my husband, the cleverest person I know.

Diolch to Mum and Aunty Bab for persevering and reading my doctoral thesis from cover to cover. Without it, there would be no book!

ENDNOTES

1. DEPARTURES

1. 'The Green, Green Grass of Home' is a song by Tom Jones. Tom Jones is one of Wales's proudest exports!

2. WHAT IS SELF-AWARENESS?

1. Mackenzie, M. M. (1988) 'The Virtues of Socratic Ignorance', *The Classical Quarterly*, 38, pp. 331–50.

2. Russo, J. E. and Schoemaker, P. J. (1992) 'Managing overconfidence', *Sloan Management Review*, 33, p. 7.

3. Fleenor, J. W., Smither, J. W., Atwater, L. E., Braddy, P. W. and Sturm, R. E. (2010) 'Self–other rating agreement in leadership: A review', *The Leadership Quarterly*, 21, pp. 1005–34.

4. Russo and Schoemaker, 'Managing overconfidence'.

5. Fenigstein, A., Scheir, M. F. and Buss, A. H. (1975) 'Public and private self-consciousness: Assessment and theory', *Journal of Consulting and Clinical Psychology*, 43, pp. 522–27.

6. Silvia, P. J. and Duval, T. S. (2001) 'Objective Self-Awareness Theory: Recent progress and enduring problems.' *Personality & Social Psychology Review (Lawrence Erlbaum Associates)*, 5, pp. 230–41.

7. Wong, C. and Law, K. S. (2002) 'The effects of leader and follower emotional intelligence on performance and attitude: An exploratory study', *The Leadership Quarterly*, 13, pp. 243–74.

8. Showry, M. and Manasa, K. V. L. (2014) 'Self-Awareness - Key to effective leadership', *IUP Journal of Soft Skills*, 8, pp. 15–26.

9. Atwater, L. E. and Yammarino, F. J. (1992) 'Does self-other agreement on leadership perceptions moderate the validity of leadership and performance predictions?' *Personnel Psychology*, 45, pp. 141–64; Van Velsor, E., Taylor, S. and Leslie, J. B. (1993a) 'An examination of the relationships among self-perception accuracy, self-awareness, gender, and leader effectiveness', *Human Resource Management*, 32, 249–63; Church, A. H. (1997) 'Managerial self-awareness in high-performing individuals in organizations', *Journal of Applied Psychology*, 82, pp. 281–92; Sosik, J. J. and Megerian, L. E. (1999) 'Understanding leader emotional intelligence and performance: The role of self-other agreement on transformational leadership perceptions', *Group & Organization Management*, 24, pp. 367–90; Bratton, V. K., Dodd, N. G. and Brown, F. W. (2011) 'The impact of emotional intelligence on accuracy of self-awareness and leadership performance', *Leadership & Organization Development Journal*, 32, pp. 127–49.

10. Fenigstein, A., Scheier, M. F. and Buss, A. H. (1975) 'Public and private self-consciousness: Assessment and theory', *Journal of Consulting and Clinical Psychology*, 43, pp. 522–27.

11. Silvia and Duval, 'Objective Self-Awareness Theory'.

12. Wong and Law, 'The effects of leader and follower emotional intelligence on performance and attitude'.

13. Showry and Manasa, 'Self-Awareness - Key to effective leadership'.

14. Ibid.

15. Riggio, R. E. and Reichard, R. J. (2008) 'The emotional and social intelligences of effective leadership: An emotional and social skill approach' *Journal of Managerial Psychology*, 23, pp. 169–85.

16. Ibid.

17. Boal, K. B. (2000). 'Strategic leadership research: Moving on', *Leadership Quarterly*, 11, p. 515.

18. Atwater and Yammarino, 'Does self-other agreement on leadership perceptions moderate the validity of leadership and performance predictions?'; Van Velsor, Taylor and Leslie, 'An examination of the relationships among self-perception accuracy, self-awareness,

gender, and leader effectiveness'; Church, 'Managerial self-awareness in high-performing individuals in organizations'; Sosik and Megerian, 'Understanding leader emotional intelligence and performance'; Bratton, Dodd and Brown, 'The impact of emotional intelligence on accuracy of self-awareness and leadership performance'.

19. McCarthy, A. M. and Garavan, T. N. (1999) 'Developing self-awareness in the managerial career development process: The value of 360-degree feedback and the MBTI', *Journal of European Industrial Training*, 23, pp. 437–45.

20. Atwater and Yammarino, 'Does self-other agreement on leadership perceptions moderate the validity of leadership and performance predictions?'; Van Velsor, Taylor and Leslie, 'An examination of the relationships among self-perception accuracy, self-awareness, gender, and leader effectiveness'; Church, 'Managerial self-awareness in high-performing individuals in organizations'; Sosik and Megerian, 'Understanding leader emotional intelligence and performance'; Bratton, Dodd and Brown, 'The impact of emotional intelligence on accuracy of self-awareness and leadership performance'.

21. Atwater and Yammarino, 'Does self-other agreement on leadership perceptions moderate the validity of leadership and performance predictions?'.

22. Kruger, J. and Dunning, D. (1999) 'Unskilled and unaware of it: How difficulties in recognizing one's own incompetence lead to inflated self-assessments', *Journal of Personality and Social Psychology*, 77, pp. 1121–34.

23. Fleenor et al., 'Self–other rating agreement in leadership'.

24. Van Velsor, Taylor and Leslie, 'An examination of the relationships among self-perception accuracy, self-awareness, gender, and leader effectiveness.'.

25. Bratton V. K. and Brown, F. W. (2011) 'The impact of emotional intelligence on accuracy of self-awareness and leadership performance', *Leadership & Organization Development Journal*, 32, 127–49.

26. Salovey, P. and Mayer, J. D. (1990) 'Emotional intelligence', *Imagination, Cognition and Personality*, 9, pp. 185–211.

27. Sosik and Megerian, 'Understanding leader emotional intelligence and performance'; Shipper, F., Kincaid, J., Rotondo, D. M. and Hoffman, R. C. (2003) 'A cross-cultural explanatory study of the linkage between emotional intelligence and managerial effectiveness', *International Journal of Organizational Analysis*, 11, pp. 171–91.

28. Shipper et al., (2003) 'A cross-cultural explanatory study of the linkage between emotional intelligence and managerial effectiveness'.

29. Ibid.

30. Valedictory Statement – Rt Hon Jacinda Ardern (5 April 2023), New Zealand Parliament, Available at https://www.parliament.nz/en/pb/hansard-debates/rhr/combined/HansDeb_20230405_20230405_44.

31. Van Velsor, Taylor and Leslie, 'An examination of the relationships among self-perception accuracy, self-awareness, gender, and leader effectiveness'; Bratton, Dodd and Brown, 'The impact of emotional intelligence on accuracy of self-awareness and leadership performance'.

32. Van Velsor, Taylor and Leslie, 'An examination of the relationships among self-perception accuracy, self-awareness, gender, and leader effectiveness'.

33. Equality and Human Rights Commission (2017) *Who runs Wales?*

3. WHAT IS LEADERSHIP?

1. George, J. M. (2000) 'Emotions and leadership: The role of emotional intelligence', *Human Relations*, 53, pp. 1027–55.

2. Parris, D. L. and Peachey, J. W. (2013) 'A systematic literature review of servant leadership theory in organizational contexts', *Journal of Business Ethics*, 113, pp. 377–93.

3. House, R. J. and Aditya, R. N. (1997) 'The social scientific study of leadership: Quo vadis?' *Journal of management*, 23, 409–73.

4. Sturm, R. E., Vera, D. and Crossan, M. (2017) 'The entanglement of leader character and leader competence and its impact on performance', *The Leadership Quarterly*, 28, 349–66.

5. Rodriguez, R. A., Green, M. T., Sun, Y. and Baggerly-Hinojosa, B.

(2017) 'Authentic leadership and transformational leadership: An incremental approach', *Journal of Leadership Studies*, 11, pp. 20–35.

6. Leslie, K. and Canwell, A. (2010) 'Leadership at all levels: Leading public sector organisations in an age of austerity', *European Management Journal*, 28, pp. 297–305.

7. Shingler-Nace, A. (2020) 'COVID-19: When leadership calls', *Nurse Leader*, 18(3), pp. 202–3.

8. Fernandez, A. A. and Shaw, G. P. (2020) 'Academic leadership in a time of crisis: The coronavirus and COVID-19', *Journal of Leadership Studies*, 14, pp. 39–45.

9. Bawafaa, E., Wong, C. A. and Laschinger, H. (2015) 'The influence of resonant leadership on the structural empowerment and job satisfaction of registered nurses', *Journal of Research in Nursing*, 20, pp. 610–22.

10. Boyatzis, R. and McKee, A. (2005) *Resonant Leadership: Renewing Yourself and Connecting with Others Through Mindfulness, Hope, and Compassion* (Boston, MA: Harvard Business Press).

11. Laschinger, H. K. S., Wong, C. A., Cummings, G. G. and Grau, A. L. (2014) 'Resonant leadership and workplace empowerment: the value of positive organizational cultures in reducing workplace incivility', *Nursing Economic$*, 32, p. 5.

12. Lenka, U. and Tiwari, B. (2016) 'Achieving triple "P" bottom line through resonant leadership: an Indian perspective', *International Journal of Productivity and Performance Management*, 65, pp. 694–703.

13. Boyatzis, R. and McKee, A. (2006) 'Inspiring others through resonant leadership', *Business Strategy Review*, 17, pp. 15–19.

14. Bass, B. M. and Bass, R. (2009) *The Bass Handbook of Leadership: Theory, Research, and Managerial Applications* (New York: Simon and Schuster); Klare, D., Behney, M. and Kenney, B. F. (2014) 'Emotional intelligence in a stupid world. Library Hi Tech News, 31, pp. 21–4.

15. Mackenzie, M. M. (1988) 'The virtues of Socratic ignorance', *The Classical Quarterly*, 38, pp. 331–50.

16. Abujbara, N. A. K. and Worley, J. (2018) 'Leading toward new horizons with soft skills', *On the Horizon*, 26, pp. 247–59.

17. Atwater, L. E., Ostroff, C., Yammarino, F. J. and Fleenor, J. W. (1998) 'Self-other agreement: Does it really matter?' *Personnel Psychology*, 51, pp. 577–98.

18. Goleman, D. (2004) 'What makes a leader?' *Harvard Business Review*, 82, pp. 82–91.

19. Showry, M. and Manasa, K. V. L. (2014) 'Self-awareness - Key to effective leadership', *IUP Journal of Soft Skills*, 8, pp. 15–26.

20. Klare, D., Behney, M. and Kenney, B. F. (2014) 'Emotional intelligence in a stupid world', *Library Hi Tech News*, 31, pp. 21–4.

21. Julie Diamond, president of Diamond Leadership, LinkedIn post, 4 August 2023.

22. Atwater and Yammarino, 1992; Van Velsor et al., 1993a; Church, 1997; Sosik and Megerian, 1999; Avolio and Gardner, 2005; Sparrowe, 2005; Barbuto and Wheeler, 2006; Lichtenstein et al., 2006; Riggio and Reichard, 2008; Bratton et al., 2011; Dinh et al., 2014; Barbuto et al., 2014; Du Plessis et al., 2015; Alavi and Gill, 2017.

23. Fleenor, J. W., Smither, J. W., Atwater, L. E., Braddy, P. W. and Sturm, R. E. (2010) 'Self–other rating agreement in leadership: A review', *The Leadership Quarterly*, 21, pp. 1005–34; Baron, L. and Parent, E. (2015) 'Developing authentic leadership within a training context: Three phenomena supporting the individual development process', *Journal of Leadership & Organizational Studies*, 22, pp. 37–53.

24. Burke, R. J. (2006) 'Why leaders fail: exploring the darkside', *International Journal of Manpower*, 27, pp. 91–100.

25. Thomas, N., (2021) *Knowing Self, Knowing Others: A Critical Exploration of Self-Awareness and Its Relevance to Leader Effectiveness Across All Levels of the Welsh Public Service.* University of South Wales (United Kingdom).

4. WHERE ARE THE LEADERS?

1. Dulewicz, V. and Higgs, M. (2003) 'Leadership at the top: The Need for Emotional Intelligence in Organizations', *The International Journal of Organizational Analysis*, 11, 193-210; Carmeli, A. (2003) 'The relationship between emotional intelligence and work attitudes,

behavior and outcomes', *Journal of Managerial Psychology*, 18, pp. 788–813; Burke, R. J. (2006) 'Why leaders fail: exploring the darkside', *International Journal of Manpower*, 27, pp. 91–100; Moorhouse, M. M. (2007) 'An exploration of emotional intelligence across career arenas', *Leadership & Organization Development Journal*, 28, pp. 296–307; Riggio, R. E. and Reichard, R. J. (2008) 'The emotional and social intelligences of effective leadership: An emotional and social skill approach' *Journal of Managerial Psychology*, 23, pp. 169–85.

2. Dulewicz and Higgs, 'Leadership at the top'.

3. Church, A. H. (1997) 'Managerial self-awareness in high-performing individuals in organizations', *Journal of Applied Psychology*, 82, pp. 281–92.

4. Dulewicz and Higgs, 'Leadership at the top'.

5. Carmeli, A. (2003) 'The relationship between emotional intelligence and work attitudes, behavior and outcomes', *Journal of Managerial Psychology*, 18, pp. 788–813.

6. Burke, 'Why leaders fail'.

7. Moorhouse, M. M. (2007) 'An exploration of emotional intelligence across career arenas', *Leadership & Organization Development Journal*, 28, pp. 296–307.

8. Rode, J. C., Arthhaud-Day, M., Ramaswami, A. and Howes, S. (2017) 'A time-lagged study of emotional intelligence and salary', *Journal of Vocational Behavior*, 101, pp. 77–89.

9. Leslie, K. and Canwell, A. (2010) 'Leadership at all levels: Leading public sector organisations in an age of austerity', *European Management Journal*, 28, pp. 297–305.

10. Lichtenstein, B. B., Uhl-Bien, M., Marion, R., Seer, A., Orton, J. D. and Schreiber, C. (2006) 'Complexity leadership theory: An interactive perspective on leading in complex adaptive systems', *E:CO Emergence: Complexity and Organization*, 8, pp. 2–12.

11. Uhl-Bien, M. and Marion, R. (2009) 'Complexity leadership in bureaucratic forms of organizing: A meso model', *The Leadership Quarterly*, 20, pp. 631–50.

12. Lichtenstein, Uhl-Bien, Marion, Seers, Orton and Schreiber 'Complexity leadership theory'.

13. Murphy, J., Rhodes, M. L., Meek, J. W. and Denyer, D. (2017) 'Managing the entanglement: Complexity leadership in public sector systems', *Public Administration Review*, 77, pp. 692–704.

14. Ibid.

15. Uhl-Bien, M. (2006) Relational leadership theory: Exploring the social processes of leadership and organizing. *The Leadership Quarterly*, 17, pp. 654–76.

16. Lichtenstein, Uhl-Bien, Marion, Seers, Orton and Schreiber, 'Complexity leadership theory'.

17. Fernandez, S., Cho, Y. J. and Perry, J. L. (2010) 'Exploring the link between integrated leadership and public sector performance', *The Leadership Quarterly*, 21, pp. 308–23.

18. Uhl-Bien and Marion, 'Complexity leadership in bureaucratic forms of organizing'.

19. Ibid.

20. Palaima, T. and Skarzauskiene, A. (2010) 'Systems thinking as a platform for leadership performance in a complex world', *Baltic Journal of Management*, 5, pp. 330–55

21. Ibid.; Boyatzis, R., Smith, M., Van Oosten, E. and Woolford, L. (2013) 'Developing resonant leaders through emotional intelligence, vision and coaching', *Organizational Dynamics*, 42, p. 17; Amdurer, E., Boyatzis, R. E., Saatcioglu, A., Smith, M. L. and Taylor, S. N. (2014) 'Long term impact of emotional, social and cognitive intelligence competencies and GMAT on career and life satisfaction and career success', *Frontiers in Psychology*, 5, p. 1447.

22. www.atlassian.com/agile/agile-at-scale/spotify

5. THE SELF-AWARENESS COMPASS

1. Fernandez, S., Cho, Y. J. and Perry, J. L. (2010) 'Exploring the link between integrated leadership and public sector performance', *The Leadership Quarterly*, 21, pp. 308–23.

2. Klare, D., Behney, M. and Kenney, B. F. (2014) 'Emotional intelligence in a stupid world', *Library Hi Tech News*, 31, pp. 21–4.

3. Van Dierendonck, D. (2011) 'Servant leadership: A review and synthesis', *Journal of Management*, 37, pp. 1228–61.

4. Morris, J. A., Brotheridge, C. M. and Urbanski, J. C. (2005) 'Bringing humility to leadership: Antecedents and consequences of leader humility', *Human Relations*, 58, pp. 1323–50.

5. Sousa, M. and Van Dierendonck, D. (2017) 'Servant leadership and the effect of the interaction between humility, action, and hierarchical power on follower engagement', *Journal of Business Ethics*, 141, pp. 13–25.

6. Ibid.; Van Dierendonck, D. and Nuijten, I. (2011) 'The servant leadership survey: Development and validation of a multidimensional measure', *Journal of Business and Psychology*, 26, pp. 249–67.

7. Avolio, B. J. and Gardner, W. L. (2005) 'Authentic leadership development: Getting to the root of positive forms of leadership', *The Leadership Quarterly*, 16, pp. 315–38.

8. Diddams, M. and Chang, G. C. (2012) 'Only human: Exploring the nature of weakness in authentic leadership', *The Leadership Quarterly*, 23, pp. 593–603.

9. Van Dierenendonck and Nuijten, 'The servant leadership survey'

10. Luthans, F., Norman, S. and Hughes, L. (2006) *Authentic Leadership*. [London: Routledge].

11. Brown, M. E. and Treviño, L. K. (2006) 'Ethical leadership: A review and future directions', *The Leadership Quarterly*, 17, pp. 595–616.

12. Walumbwa, F.O., Avolio, B.J., Gardner, W.L., Wernsing, T.S. and Peterson, S.J. (2008) 'Authentic leadership: Development and validation of a theory-based measure', *Journal of management*, 34(1), pp.89-126.

13. Sparrowe, R. T. (2005) 'Authentic leadership and the narrative self', *The Leadership Quarterly*, 16, 419–39.

14. Bass, B. M. and Bass, R. (2009) *The Bass Handbook of Leadership: Theory, Research, and Managerial Applications* (New York: Simon and Schuster).

15. Hoch, J. E., Bommer, W. H., Dulebohn, J. H. and Wu, D. (2016) 'Do ethical, authentic, and servant leadership explain variance above and beyond transformational leadership? A meta-analysis', *Journal of Management*, 44(2), pp. 501–29.

16. Walumbwa, F. O., Avolio, B. J., Gardner, W. L., Wernsing, T. S. and Peterson, S. J. (2008) 'Authentic leadership: Development and validation of a theory-based measure', *Journal of Management*, 34, pp. 89–126.

17. Sparrowe, 'Authentic leadership and the narrative self'.

18. Bass and Bass, *The Bass Handbook of Leadership*.

19. Alavi, S. B. and Gill, C. (2017) 'Leading change authentically: How authentic leaders influence follower responses to complex change', *Journal of Leadership & Organizational Studies*, 24, pp. 157–71.

20. Church, A. H. (1997) 'Managerial self-awareness in high-performing individuals in organizations', Journal of Applied Psychology, 82, pp. 281–92; Kondrat, M. E. (1999) 'Who is the "self" in self-aware?: Professional self-awareness from a critical theory perspective', *Social Service Review*, 73, pp. 451–77; Silvia, P. J. and Duval, T. S. (2001) 'Objective self-awareness theory: Recent progress and enduring problems', *Personality & Social Psychology Review (Lawrence Erlbaum Associates)*, 5, pp. 230–41; Sparrowe, 'Authentic leadership and the narrative self'; Morgan, G. (2009) 'Reflective practice and self-awareness', *Perspectives in Public Health*, 129, pp. 161–2.

21. Freshwater, D. (2002) *Therapeutic Nursing: Improving Patient Care Through Self-Awareness and Reflection* (London, SAGE Publications Ltd).

22. Du Plessis, M., Wakelin, Z. and Nel, P. (2015) 'The influence of emotional intelligence and trust on servant leadership', *SA Journal of Industrial Psychology*, 41, pp. 1–9.

23. Bass and Bass, *The Bass Handbook of Leadership*.

24. Burke, R. J. (2006) 'Why leaders fail: exploring the darkside', *International Journal of Manpower*, 27, pp. 91–100; Sturm, R. E., Vera, D. and Crossan, M. (2017) 'The entanglement of leader character and leader competence and its impact on performance', *The Leadership Quarterly*, 28, pp. 349–66.

25. Caldwell, C. (2009) 'Identity, self-awareness, and self-deception: Ethical implications for leaders and organizations.' *Journal of Business Ethics*, 90, pp. 393–406.

26. Murphy, J., Rhodes, M. L., Meek, J. W. and Denyer, D. (2017) 'Managing the entanglement: Complexity leadership in public sector systems', *Public Administration Review*, 77, pp. 692–704.

27. Petrie, N. (2011) 'Future trends in leadership development', *Center for Creative Leadership white paper*, 5(5), p. 36.

28. Hogan, R., Curphy, G. J. and Hogan, J. (1994) 'What we know about leadership: Effectiveness and personality', *American Psychologist*, 49, p. 493; Shipper, F. and Dillard, J. (2000) 'A study of impending derailment and recovery of middle managers across career stages', *Human Resource Management*, 39, pp. 331–45; Sparrowe, 'Authentic leadership and the narrative self'; Gray, D. and Jones, K. (2018) 'The resilience and wellbeing of public sector leaders', *International Journal of Public Leadership*, 14, pp. 138–54.

29. Academi Wales (2017) *Leading in the Welsh Public Service – A Leadership Behaviours Framework for Senior Leaders* [Online]. OGL Crown Copyright. Available: tinyurl.com/49tb62k3 (p. 4).

30. Gray and Jones (2018) 'The resilience and wellbeing of public sector leaders'.

31. Sosik, J. J. and Megerian, L. E. (1999) 'Understanding leader emotional intelligence and performance: The role of self-other agreement on transformational leadership perceptions', *Group & Organization Management*, 24, pp. 367–90.

32. Van Velsor, E., Taylor, S. and Leslie, J. B. (1993) 'An Examination of the Relationships among Self-Perception Accuracy, Self-Awareness, Gender, and Leader Effectiveness', *Human Resource Management*, 32, 249–63.

6. SIGNPOSTS AND DIRECTIONS

1. Sosik, J. J. and Megerian, L. E. (1999) 'Understanding leader emotional intelligence and performance: The role of self-other agreement on transformational leadership perceptions', *Group & Organization Management*, 24, pp. 367–90.

2. Van Velsor, E., Taylor, S. and Leslie, J.B. (1993) 'An examination of the relationships among self-perception accuracy, self-awareness, gender, and leader effectiveness', *Human Resource Management*, 32(2-3), pp.249–263.

3. Uhl-Bien, M. and Marion, R. (2009) 'Complexity leadership in bureaucratic forms of organizing: A meso model' *The Leadership Quarterly*, 20, pp. 631–50.

4. George, J. M. (2000) 'Emotions and leadership: The role of emotional intelligence', *Human Relations*, 53, pp. 1027–55.

5. Fernandez, S., Cho, Y. J. and Perry, J. L. (2010) 'Exploring the link between integrated leadership and public sector performance', *The Leadership Quarterly*, 21, pp. 308–23.

7. ROADBLOCKS AND TRIP HAZARDS

1. Sturm, R. E., Vera, D. and Crossan, M. (2017) 'The entanglement of leader character and leader competence and its impact on performance', *The Leadership Quarterly*, 28, pp. 349–66.

2. Boyatzis, R., Smith, M., Van Oosten, E. and Woolford, L. (2013) 'Developing resonant leaders through emotional intelligence, vision and coaching', *Organizational Dynamics*, 42, p. 17.

3. Gray, D. and Jones, K. (2018) 'The resilience and wellbeing of public sector leaders', *International Journal of Public Leadership*, 14, pp. 138–54.

4. Wright, B. E. and Pandey, S. K. (2009) 'Transformational leadership in the public sector: Does structure matter?', *Journal of Public Administration Research and Theory*, 20, pp. 75–89; Van der Voet, J. (2014) 'The effectiveness and specificity of change management in a public organization: Transformational leadership and a bureaucratic organizational structure', *European Management Journal*, 32, pp. 373–82.

5. Uhl-Bien, M. and Marion, R. (2009) 'Complexity leadership in bureaucratic forms of organizing: A meso model', *The Leadership Quarterly*, 20, pp. 631–50; Wright, B. E. and Pandey, S. K. (2009) 'Transformational leadership in the public sector: Does structure matter?', *Journal of Public Administration Research and Theory*, 20,

pp. 75–89; Murphy, J., Rhodes, M. L., Meek, J. W. and Denyer, D. (2017) 'Managing the entanglement: Complexity leadership in public sector systems', *Public Administration Review*, 77, pp. 692–704.

6. Allen, T. W. (2012) 'Confronting complexity and creating unity of effort: The leadership challenge for public administrators', *Public Administration Review*, 72, pp. 320–1.

7. Ibid.

8. Needham, C. and Mangan, C. (2014) 'The 21st century public servant', *Birmingham: University of Birmingham*.

9. Fernandez, A. A. and Shaw, G. P. (2020) 'Academic leadership in a time of crisis: The coronavirus and COVID-19', *Journal of Leadership Studies*, 14, pp. 39–45.

10. Boyatzis, R. and McKee, A. (2005) *Resonant Leadership: Renewing Yourself and Connecting with Others Through Mindfulness, Hope, and Compassion* (Boston, MA: Harvard Business Press).

11. Rochat, P. (2003) 'Five levels of self-awareness as they unfold early in life', *Consciousness and Cognition*, 12, pp. 717–31.

12. George, J. M. (2000) 'Emotions and leadership: The role of emotional intelligence', *Human Relations*, 53, pp. 1027–55.

13. Boyatzis, R. and McKee, A. (2006) 'Inspiring others through resonant leadership', *Business Strategy Review*, 17, pp. 15–19.

14. Boyatzis, Smith, Van Oosten and Woolford, 'Developing resonant leaders through emotional intelligence, vision and coaching'.

15. Lenka, U. and Tiwari, B. (2016) 'Achieving triple "P" bottom line through resonant leadership: an Indian perspective', *International Journal of Productivity and Performance Management*, 65, pp. 694–703.

16. Shingler-Nace, A. (2020) 'COVID-19: When leadership calls', *Nurse Leader*, 18(3), pp. 202–203.

17. Fernandez and Shaw, 'Academic leadership in a time of crisis'.

18. Ibid.

19. Ibid.

8. TRAVEL GUIDES

1. Maul, A., Torres Irribarra, D. and Wilson, M. (2016) 'On the philosophical foundations of psychological measurement', *Measurement*, 79, pp. 311–20.

2. Babones, S. (2016) 'Interpretive quantitative methods for the social sciences', *Sociology*, 50, pp. 453–69.

3. Maul, Torres Irribarra and Wilson, 'On the philosophical foundations of psychological measurement'.

4. Michell, J. (2011) 'Qualitative research meets the ghost of Pythagoras', *Theory & Psychology*, 21, pp. 241–59.

5. Guyon, H., Kop, J., Juhel, J. and Falissard, B. (2018) 'Measurement, ontology, and epistemology: Psychology needs pragmatism-realism', *Theory & Psychology*, 28, pp. 149–71.

6. Michell, 'Qualitative research meets the ghost of Pythagoras'.

7. Ibid.

8. On, Bar, and R. Bar On Emotional Quotient Inventory. "Technical manual." *Toronto: Multi Health Systems* (1997).

9. Parker, J. D. A., Keefer, K. V. and Wood, L. M. (2011) 'Toward a brief multidimensional assessment of emotional intelligence: Psychometric properties of the emotional quotient inventory-short form', *Psychological Assessment*, 23, pp. 762–77.

10. Salovey, P., Mayer, J. D., Goldman, S. L., Turvey, C., and Palfai, T. P. (1995) 'Emotional attention, clarity, and repair: Exploring emotional intelligence using the Trait Meta-Mood Scale', In J. W. Pennebaker (Ed.), *Emotion, disclosure, & health* (pp. 125–154). American Psychological Association.

11. Petrides, K.V. (2009) 'Psychometric properties of the trait emotional intelligence questionnaire (TEIQue)', In *Assessing emotional intelligence: Theory, research, and applications* (pp. 85-101). Boston, MA: Springer US.

12. Avolio, B.J. and Bass, B.M., 2004. *Multifactor Leadership Questionnaire: Manual & Review Copy*. Mind Garden.

13. Rodiguez, R. A., Green, M. T., Sun, Y. and Baggerly-Hinojosa, B. (2017) 'Authentic leadership and transformational leadership: An

incremental approach', *Journal of Leadership Studies*, 11, pp. 20–35.

14. Schriesheim, C. A., Wu, J. B. and Scandura, T. A. (2009) 'A meso measure? Examination of the levels of analysis of the Multifactor Leadership Questionnaire (MLQ)', *The Leadership Quarterly*, 20, pp. 604–16.

15. Walumbwa, F. O., Avolio, B. J., Gardner, W. L., Wernsing, T. S. and Peterson, S. J. (2008) 'Authentic leadership: Development and validation of a theory-based measure', *Journal of Management*, 34, pp. 89–126.

16. Duncan, P., Green, M., Gergen, E. and Ecung, W. (2017) 'Authentic leadership--Is it more than emotional intelligence?', *Administrative Issues Journal: Connecting Education, Practice, and Research*, 7, pp. 11–22.

17. Cummings, G. (2006) 'Hospital restructuring and nursing leadership: a journey from research question to research program', *Nursing Administration Quarterly*, 30, pp. 321–9.

18. Cummings, G. (2004) 'Investing relational energy: the hallmark of resonant leadership', *Nursing Leadership (Toronto, Ont.)*, 17, pp. 76–87.

19. Cummings, G.G., Grau, A.L. and Wong, C.A. (2014) 'Resonant leadership and workplace empowerment: The value of positive organizational cultures in reducing workplace incivility', *Nursing*, 32(1), p. 6.